Thinking Like Jesus

Dr. Ray Guarendi

Thinking Like Jesus

The Psychology of a Faithful Disciple

EWTN PUBLISHING, INC.
Irondale, Alabama

EWTN Publishing, Inc.
5817 Old Leeds Road, Irondale, AL 35210

Distributed by Sophia Institute Press, Box 5284, Manchester, NH 03108.

Library of Congress Cataloging-in-Publication Data

Names: Guarendi, Ray, author.
Title: Thinking like Jesus : the psychology of a faithful disciple / Dr. Ray
   Guarendi.
Description: Irondale, Alabama : EWTN Publishing, Inc., 2018.
Identifiers: LCCN 2018022296 | ISBN 9781682780626 (pbk. : alk. paper)
Subjects: LCSH: Christianity—Psychology. | Christianity—Philosophy.
Classification: LCC BR110 .G795 2018 | DDC 248.4—dc23 LC record available at https://lccn.loc.gov/2018022296

To Father Kevin Fete:
May his soul rest in peace.

Contents

Thinking Like Jesus

1

Willing the How

How can I be nicer to my annoying sister-in-law? How can I discipline my kids more calmly? How can I control my temper? How can I lose this excess weight? How can I pray more?

Note how each question begins: "How?" It asks for techniques, strategies, methods. What do I need to do to bring about the desired result?

Parents ask me in similar language: What's the best way to motivate my son? How do I stop all the sibling bickering? What should I do to become more consistent? The phrasing reveals the goal: What are the steps to make this happen?

Therapy does a lot of good for a lot of people. But it has sent an unintended message to the culture at large — that we now have the ability to fix most any problem and to make life better. Witness the near universal advocacy for therapy to ameliorate almost every sort of struggle or personal turmoil.

If life lent itself so readily to formulas of action or to therapeutic prescriptions, then the smartest, most knowledgeable people would be the most well-adjusted. They would be the most able to figure out the proper prescriptions to contented living. Intelligence doesn't necessarily equate to *resolve*.

Thinking Like Jesus

Always asking "How?" is asking for frustration. If there is a *how*, then I can find it. If I can find it, then I can apply it. If I can apply it, then what I want to happen should happen. If it doesn't, I question, "What's wrong? What am I missing?"

Are there better and worse ways to solve troubles? Obviously. Otherwise, there would be no reason to listen to anyone's advice. (And psychologists would have little to offer anybody.) Are there better ways to be kind to an obnoxious relative? Better ways to discipline a child, and not something easier, like a timber wolf? Smarter ideas for weight loss? Yes to all. A fundamental for good living has been displaced, however, by an expanding emphasis on the *how*. That fundamental is *the will*.

God says we are made in His image. In part, that means that we have, though not at His infinite level, intellect and will. Will is the down-deep determination to be pleasant to my sister-in-law, to lose weight, to stay calm. It is the part of me that determines to act better, with God's will strengthening mine. "How-tos" help, but first comes the will to use them.

A famous shoe company's slogan is "Just do it." Though meant for athletes, it is great advice for Christians. So much of how we are to live builds upon the will to just do it.

"Do you want to be here?" A question I ask clients. Obviously, they do: After all, they came in. That's only the beginning step. The next, and most helpful, steps are to go where the counseling leads — in other words, to do the work of self-improvement. Many come to therapy hoping for some kind of "how-tos" for making their marriage, parenting, or mood better. Though we talk about ideas and methods, without the will to take those from the office into life, nothing happens.

When parents ask me discipline questions, I can usually give them several options. What I can't give is the will to follow through. They know what to do; they need to do what they know.

Willing the How

Suppose an elderly family member is in the latter stages of dementia and resides in a skilled nursing facility. She no longer recognizes family; her words are chaotic and near meaningless; and she is prone to outbursts of cursing. Certainly she's not the person you knew growing up, and to spend time with her would be disheartening. She's different now, and it's not easy to accept. Your head says, "Go see her"; but your heart says, "It hurts."

How (there's that word again) do you conquer your qualms? How do you get past your resistance? Simple: You go. You "just do it." You don't scour your mind for quasi-therapeutic techniques to become more settled before venturing through the door. You act. Your first *how* is simply traveling from your place to hers. You get in your car, drive, walk into the building, head to her room, and visit with her. Your will to do good is what moves you, not some knowledge of how to resolve whatever cauldron of emotions might be inhibiting you. What's more, your emotions will settle by acting counter to them. You won't have to exert quite so much will. Doing good strengthens the will.

For the past forty years I have lifted weights. (That's right: I was the only kid in first grade who worked out.) The faces in the exercise room are fairly familiar, except after the first of January. A wave of new people enters, ready to get in better shape. A newcomer might ask me, "How can I stay at it?" My answer is, "Just show up." No question, some days it will seem nearly impossible to muster the motivation to walk the treadmill, lift the weights, hit the machines. The strategies to make yourself get there are few. You just need to show up. The initial inertia of, "It's just so much easier to stay home," will be overcome by the will. The actual exercising—the *how* of losing weight and getting in shape—naturally will follow.

How can I be nicer to my hard-to-like sister-in-law? Answer: Be nicer. How can I discipline my kids more calmly? Answer: Don't yell. How do I lose this excess weight? Answer: Eat healthier and exercise. How can I pray more? Answer: Pray more.

Psychologists live in the world of "How?" My work involves finding ways to help someone, no matter what he's grappling with. The search for hows has reinforced for me the need for the will. Without the will, "How?" is an intellectual exercise. Christianity understood this long before the arrival of modern how-to thinking.

2

No Need to Forgive

Truly, truly, I say to you, unless you eat the flesh of the Son of man and drink his blood, you have no life in you.... He who eats my flesh and drinks my blood abides in me, and I in him." ... Many of his disciples, when they heard it, said, "This is a hard saying; who can listen to it?" ... After this many of his disciples drew back and no longer went about with him." (John 6:53, 56, 60, 66)

Jesus taught much that outraged people of His time. The most radical and hardest lesson to swallow was that His followers were to eat and drink His actual flesh and blood. Unless one is predisposed by grace, then and now, who indeed can listen to it?

Jesus gave another saying that was hard to listen to, much less follow. "Then Peter came up and said to him, 'Lord, how often shall my brother sin against me, and I forgive him? As many as seven times?' Jesus said to him, 'I do not say to you seven times, but seventy times seven'" (Matt. 18:21–22).

By suggesting seven times, Peter was actually raising the bar set by some rabbis, who said that three times was enough. Perhaps Peter wanted to show Jesus how well he was absorbing this new teaching on mercy. Jesus answered by raising the bar to the limit: Not literally 490 times, but completely and always.

Completely? Always? Is there some way I can get an exemption here or there? My disagreeable relative, my overbearing boss, my prickly neighbor, most anyone whom I think I should forgive: Do I have to do so all the time? Can I find some looseness in Christ's teaching? Well, *psychologically speaking*, maybe.

A scenario: My wife calls her mother to watch the children on an evening she'll be out, but I'll be home. Given my touchiness about being thought a mediocre caregiver (They need fed? When?), I confront my wife for making me look inept to her mother.

After reminding me that I'm the child needing the most supervision (which I admit) and that she had originally planned to ask our ten-year-old daughter to supervise me, she says her actual intent was to give me some free time to write my parenting book. (Is that supposed to make me feel better?)

Conclusions? First, I misread my wife's motives. Second, I took offense based on that misreading. Third, I was *ready* to be charitable and to forgive. And fourth, I had nothing to forgive, as she did *nothing wrong*. This was not a seventy-times-seven occasion.

How many times have I struggled to overlook someone's offense against me and to forgive, thinking myself pretty magnanimous, when in fact the offense existed only in my head? It was my misinterpretation, my oversensitivity, my vigilance to personal slight that convinced me I was "sinned" against. I'm glad I don't know the number of times I've done this. I do know it's more than seventy times seven.

Therapists have to listen hard and long to uncover motives. The client himself often doesn't understand why he does what he does. Most motives are a mix of known and unknown, good and bad, selfless and selfish. Fathoming it all can take hours of therapy.

No Need to Forgive

In most circumstances, we judge others' motives immediately. On the spot we assess what exactly was meant and why. Our mind analyzes others' words as soon as they are spoken, with an accuracy that lies anywhere between 100 and 0 percent.

Reading intent is quite tricky, and prone to error. We can hear words and see behavior, but we can't peer inside someone's head. Yet we routinely do so and react accordingly. What we think is intent can raise or lower our emotional temperature. Words uttered with apparent calculation hit a lot harder than words spoken thoughtlessly.

Your mother remarks that you are a much stricter disciplinarian than she ever was. Because she has said similar things in the past, you hear a put-down. Truth is, one of her motherhood regrets is that she was too lax. Though it didn't sound this way to you, she was indirectly complimenting you. Her apparent criticism of you was actually criticism of herself.

After stewing from the "sting" for two and a half hours, you pray, asking God to settle you down. On this occasion, though, your need to settle was wrapped around nothing. It was hanging in psychological midair.

Seventy times seven. Fully, honestly, always. It's doable only with God's help. But you can help yourself, too. You may not need to forgive as much as you think. Just make certain there is really something to forgive and not something only in your mind's eye or ear.

3

It's My Nature

A college student asked me, "Do you think children by nature are cooperative?" In full psychologist mode, I asked her back, "What do you think?" She replied, "I think children are more willful than cooperative, but my professor says the opposite. He put this question on our exam, and he's made it clear in class what answer he expects." "How uncooperative," I thought.

Her professor obviously believes Christianity is fundamentally wrong about human nature. (One might ask: How is a faithful Christian student to honestly answer the question and still pass?) Indeed, modern child development teaches that children innately are inclined to cooperate. Christianity teaches that cooperation doesn't come naturally. It has to be taught.

G. K. Chesterton, a keen-eyed social commentator—and one who clearly never took child-development classes—observed that the one Christian doctrine with abundant empirical evidence is that of original sin. We begin and end life with a bent toward self.

To be fair, not all theorists downplay the idea of original sin, though they might not use that term. For instance, a psychologist named Albert Ellis developed a counseling approach he called Rational Emotive Therapy. He maintained that to change distressing emotions, we need to change our thinking. We need to look at ourselves and our lives in more rational, less self-defeating ways. Unfortunately, we have a tendency toward "stinking thinking," as he put it. And this tendency is buried deep in our wiring as human beings. Hmmm ...

Ponder the personality of the prototypical toddler: He's impulsive, wanting what he wants the instant he wants it. If thwarted, he will let it be known to all—with intensity, emotion, and decibels. He disagrees instinctively with Copernicus—he, not the sun, is the center of the solar system. What are among his earliest words? "Me," "No," "No want to." What two-year-old has to be instructed, "Now remember, Charity, don't share your toys. They're all yours." When facing discipline, does Ernest comply by saying, "Don't forget, Father. Set the timer, and feel free to take a nap. I won't leave the corner until I hear it ding."

Christian parents know up close and personal about original sin. Their children remind them every day. Yet they resort to descriptions that seem to agree with child-development professors.

"He is so strong-willed." (Synonyms: oppositional, contrary, stubborn, and determined.)

"She's a challenge."

"She's seven going on seventeen."

"He's high-maintenance."

"He's a difficult child."

One mother quipped, "'Difficult child' is redundant."

All these adjectives suggest that the child in question is tougher than typical. If, however, being willful is more or less normal, then being "strong-willed" is also more or less normal. It would be more accurate to say "normal-willed"—or, simply, "child."

Of course, kids run the continuum of cooperativeness, differing in how readily they absorb guidance. Some really do seem to glide along smoothly with their parents. Such youngsters are not the rule, but they do exist. I once read about a family in Nova Scotia who has three of them. I'm still waiting on independent corroboration.

Suppose your first child is a Harmony or an Oxford—a more cooperative, or, better to say, less willful offspring. She's normal, right? In fact, God gave you a practice round, a parenting mulligan. He said, "Here, play with this. I'll send the real kid later." No matter how easy Harmony is to raise, she still shares her nature with all humans. Also, she's not a teen yet.

Would that children were more eager to cooperate. A parent wouldn't need to assert much authority or to teach responsibility and morals. She could just reason like Socrates, reflect feelings like a therapist, and design a state-of-the-art sticker reward chart. Whereupon, Spike would grasp her hand, singing "Kumbaya" as both strolled through family life in one accord.

Sounds nice, doesn't it? But the truth is that no matter how savvy the parenting, almost all children will resist, whether a little or a lot.

Suppose I am convinced that Chuckie is some wild little hellion who demands superhuman patience and perseverance to raise. Feeling overwhelmed, my exasperation soars and my sense of being a saintly parent plummets. On the other hand, it would likely be more realistic to see him as a typical, push-the-limits child. His willfulness is part of who he is, and not necessarily an aberration from the norm. Put as a question, who is harder to enjoy: a child you think is "normal," or one you think is unusually tough?

The more a parent sees a child as far too challenging, the more she's likely to take his conduct personally. "Why does he act this way? Is he trying to make my life difficult? Why can't he be more agreeable?" Little Will may not be deliberately seeking to make Mom's or Dad's days twenty-five hours long. He is just doing what comes naturally: acting undisciplined.

Thinking Like Jesus

The good news: Willfulness is a quality that pushes a parent to reach deeper inside for more patience, perseverance, consistency, and affection. The natural ways of children push us to supernatural virtues.

4

Beyond First Impressions

"He seemed like such a nice guy. Always waved to me when he drove by. We had a cookout last week, and he came over and gave us a dozen ears of corn. This doesn't seem to fit with what I know of him now."

So says the shocked neighbor to the probing eyes of television cameras seeking reasons why this "nice guy" has just been arrested for breaking into seven homes two streets away.

Parents diagnose "Jekyll-Hyde" when describing how little Conan is a barbarian at home, but in public, "everybody compliments us on him, telling us what a great kid he is."

They sit bewildered at school as the teacher regales, "What a delight he is in class! He is just so likeable." Hearing this, dad pulls a picture from his wallet, asking, "Is this the child? What school is this? Who are you?"

A high-profile religious personality who presents himself as a faithful son of the Church is ultimately revealed to be a fraud. Much to his admirers' dismay, he leads a life contrary to his image.

All of these follow one theme: I thought I knew this person. Now I don't know what to think. Could I have been that mistaken?

Thinking Like Jesus

How does one reconcile the contrasting pictures: nice neighbor versus thief; defiant home child versus angelic school child; holy preacher versus unholy lifestyle? Well, they don't necessarily need to be reconciled. All are human, and therefore all are complex beings. Conan is not one person with his parents and another with Mrs. Gradehard. The preacher's words aren't false, though he might not be living them. The burglar really is a sociable man at neighborhood barbecues. All are responding to distinct environments with distinct temptations. Different places promote different conduct. So do different people.

Aren't there different people in your life who evoke very different sides of you? Your favorite brother-in-law is likeable and easy to be around; he naturally makes you feel relaxed in his presence. "Uneasy" would be the last word he'd use to describe you.

Your other brother-in-law can be contrary and opinionated. Around him you are uncomfortable and don't hide it very well. He sees you as an ill-at-ease person.

Which brother-in-law is right about you? Both would be surprised to hear the other's portrayal. Which is the real you? Well, both, depending on whom you're with.

Don't people put up façades — that is, crafted images of themselves to hide ulterior motives or to gain accolades? Sure, but "false fronts" aren't always bad. Christians must regularly talk or act counter to how their urges would dictate. It's called charity, and at times it has to be forced. That doesn't mean it's not genuine.

To describe others, we use "trait language," condensing a lot of impressions and experience down to summary words. When I call someone "pleasant," I'm really saying, "From what I know of him across all the situations I've seen him in, more often than not he acts pleasantly." Now, nobody talks like this — well, except psychologists.

"She's nice; he's a braggart; she's touchy; he's generous." We talk in broad terms. It's universal to humans—a trait, if you will.

As a consequence, once we settle on a characteristic, we tend to see the person consistently in that light. So, when she says or does something contrary to it, we not only are surprised but may feel any of a range of other reactions—disappointment, dismay, disillusion, even betrayal. Any of these can provoke ill feelings, which are based on an incomplete understanding of personality.

Even professional people-readers are inclined toward quick and durable impressions. One study found that clinicians formed a diagnosis within the first several minutes of an interview, persisting with it even in the face of other contradictory information.

Someone might compliment me after a parenting presentation: "You must be a great dad." I'm tempted to respond, "I hope so, but you can't know that. I may have sounded good the past hour, but that doesn't mean I act so at home." Instead, I say something like, "Thanks, but you'll have to ask my wife and kids about that. They live with me." Anything more would sound too shrink-like. If they said, "I'll bet you're a good dad," though, I might just let it go. At least they're making a bet: They recognize the chance they might be wrong.

Shouldn't we give others the benefit of the doubt? Aren't we supposed to see the best in people? We can do both, yet still be accurate in our judgments. In fact, it is more loving to recognize both the sweet and the sour, the pretty and the ugly in another—and to love them through it all. I have little problem loving the "saints" in my life. It's the sinners (all of us) who can push my mercy to its edges. I don't want to have to downplay someone's sins to enable myself to love them better. I'm called to love, even as someone's faults become more apparent to me.

Of all the people in our lives, only a relative handful do we know in depth. The rest (including celebrities and other public persons) we know about an inch deep. Having listened to the media preacher speaking faithfully and forcefully many times, we think, "He's a holy man." He may well be. Most are. But to conclude with absolute certainty that he is indeed as holy as he sounds is setting oneself up for disillusionment. One too many instances of disillusionment can lead to cynicism.

Is it smarter, then, to take a "wait and see" view of others, always mindful that they might not be who they appear? Our Faith says that it's not so simple as that. It says to love what they appear to be *and* whatever they eventually show themselves to be. A fact of any relationship: The more you come to know someone, the more you'll come to know their sins. And they will come to know yours.

Never be surprised when someone acts counter to your image of him. With continued contact, that will happen more often, making him either easier or harder to love. The further a friend deviates from our previous image of him, the further we'll have to reach to think charitably of him.

It's a truth of psychology: We don't really know most people. It's a truth of Christianity: We are to love what we know, whether we know a little or a lot.

5

Holy or Jerk?

Some decades back I turned away from the Catholic Church and moved into an independent evangelical congregation. In our Bible study, a recurrent question was this: Why do others get upset with us as Christians, particularly about our moral principles? A recurrent answer: Our principles convict them. Somewhere down deep they know we're right.

No question, to be Christian is to be misunderstood. Our Lord said, "If they persecuted me, they will persecute you" (John 15:20). Strong moral stances do threaten others, all the more so if God is quoted as their author. Still flickering inside them is a God-placed sense of right and wrong. Theologians call it the natural law.

For me, though, that Bible study question raised more questions: Is it my convictions that rankle others, or might it be something less virtuous? Do they see me as authentically "holy," or just "holier than thou"? Bluntly put, "Am I holy or a jerk?"

This is not to suggest compromising one's morals to get along. It is to emphasize that when talking or acting morally, I need to squelch any unspoken attitude that signals, "You're not as good as I am"; or "I'm looking down on you"; or "I'm not the sinner you are." One can be morally upright and still be a jerk about it.

Fair or not, others will call us out if our words don't fit our behavior.

The second car stopped at a traffic light is adorned with bumper stickers: "My boss is a Jewish carpenter"; "Know Jesus, know peace"; "John 3:16." The signal turns green, and the first car just sits there. Within one-half second, the second driver leans on his horn, wildly waving his arms, to no result. The light returns to red. At the next green, there still is no movement from the first car, and its driver looks to be texting. Fuming, the second driver starts to pound on his steering wheel while screaming and cursing through his open window.

Behind both cars idles a police cruiser, the officer witnessing the whole episode. Flashing lights appear, and the officer strides to the window: "Please pull over and follow me to my car." Enraged, the driver fires off, "What?! You can't detain me for screaming in my own car!" "I'm not," replies the officer. "I'm going to check your ID and plates. I suspect you stole this car from a Christian."

Restaurant servers tell of watching customers pray a meal blessing and afterward leave little or no tip. (I up my standard tip by 50 percent if my server sees me praying, 75 percent if two see it.) Or sometimes the praying customers are demanding and rude, leaving a bad taste in the server's mouth about "religious" people.

Family and friends are acutely aware of our standards, and they are nearby to notice our falling short of them. What's more, if they think we think we're superior people, they'll find a way to needle us: "I guess that's just how a Christian talks." "And she calls herself a good Catholic." "I thought you were the religious one."

What's the best thing we can give to those who matter most to us? Most don't need shelter, food, money, or physical care. Our gift is our personality, specifically its better side. We can make the effort to be winsome, to show interest in them and their lives, to be pleasant and agreeable, and to be less self-focused and more them-focused. Of all people, we should be among the most appealing and easiest to be around.

Not uncommonly, two spouses are separated faith-wise. One embraces it with zeal, while the other is lukewarm at best, resistant at worst. How can the more faithful move the less faithful? She can demonstrate that love for Christ simply makes them better—more affectionate, more giving, more forgiving, less irritable, less argumentative. (I know, a long list.) Prodding, preaching, or an attitude of spiritual superiority doesn't win over anyone. Her spouse may not be as averse to Christianity as he is to feeling viewed as religiously stunted.

One needn't sacrifice moral truth to be likeable. Family, especially grown children who are living morally at odds with their upbringing, have long known your convictions. More preaching may just push them further away. Strive to show them that your faith-guided life, if at all possible, will not cause unnecessary friction between you and them.

If God's truth makes others feel unsettled, then good. The spark of the Divine may yet inflame them. I can't alter God's teaching to make someone feel comfortable. The last thing I want to do, however, is to communicate a superior attitude, or to conduct myself in a way that betrays the faith I claim. My prayer: God help me to be holy, not a jerk.

6

Learning from Pop

My father was born a few years before the Great Depression. His boyhood, like that of many in his Italian neighborhood, was family-centered and materially modest. As a freshman, he entered McKinley High School in Canton, Ohio, where a young girl named Rita Rizzo was a senior. Later called to religious life, Rita took the name Angelica and eventually founded the Eternal Word Television Network (EWTN). My dad and Rita likely crossed paths at their parish, St. Anthony's. As a boy, I wondered if there was some law that required Italian Catholics to attend St. Anthony's.

During his sophomore year, Pop left school to work full-time. All his checks went straight to his mother to help support the family. Would a teen nowadays even tithe 10 percent to his parents?

Eventually my father was hired at a machine shop, where he worked for forty-three years, never missing a day for the last thirteen. At 5:30 every morning he headed to a loud, hot, smelly factory. His job was physically exhausting, but he never groused about it. He knew it allowed him to raise his family and put four children through college, an education few in his generation reached. At age fifty-nine, Pop achieved a lingering lifelong goal by getting his G.E.D. Far and away the oldest in his class, he was also the most excited.

Thinking Like Jesus

My father lived a quietly Catholic life. He never missed Mass, saw that we were taught the Faith, received the sacraments, and learned morals. When I left the Catholic Church in my thirties, Pop was puzzled and disappointed, but he never let his connection to me weaken.

Shortly after retiring, Pop was hit with a health double-whammy —diabetes and heart failure. You wouldn't know about his diabetes unless you saw the insulin shot. As his heart progressively exhausted itself, when he was asked how he felt, his standard comeback was a "so-so" wobble of his hand. Once he confessed to me, "I feel poohed." That was his idea of complaining.

On the night before he died, my brother and I were helping him to his bed. He said, "When I feel a little better, I've got to get back to lifting and get some of my strength back." He wasn't denying his impending death; he just wanted to give his boys some hope.

So why this trip through my father's life? When parents give much of themselves, learning from them continues beyond childhood and after their passing. Grown-up eyes see what child eyes miss. Qualities in my father that slipped past me then, I now appreciate. He seldom complained, even when he understandably could have.

Gratefulness has an antagonist: complaining. The more words of complaint, the fewer words of gratitude. Our fallen humanity is inclined to spend more time occupied with what's going wrong than what's going right.

Complaints emerge from a mindset: Life is not acting as I would wish. I know how I would like things to go. Should they refuse to cooperate, I can feel frustrated, dismayed, betrayed.

A complaint is a constricted view of things. It fails to see life through a wider lens, ideally through a God-lens. The complaint ignores the broader reality.

My foot gives me constant trouble; I can walk.

The air conditioning went out again last week; I have shelter.
My boss is obnoxious; I have a job.
Our priest isn't friendly; I'm a Catholic.
This is my third operation; I can be cured.
Are these necessarily complaints? When I talk about my aching feet, lousy job, exasperating kids, couldn't I just be making conversation, sharing a little of my life? Sure. There is a difference, though, between describing "what is" and "what is unfair." And it's not all that hard to hear it.

Tone. What words mean can be turned upside down by their tone. A tone can say, "My job stinks. I deserve a whole lot better." It speaks to a grievance about someone or something, one I shouldn't have to endure.

Parents know firsthand the chafing power of tone. Whining has been likened to the sound of a buzz saw hitting a rusty nail, or listening to acid-rock music during a root canal. They repeatedly admonish, "Don't whine." Whining is not appealing to anyone of any age. The kids, though, have an excuse. They're kids. Whining from an adult is, well … how rusty is that nail?

One antidote to a complaining tone is self-listening. How am I sounding right now? What words am I using? Am I whining? Complaints tend to feed upon themselves. My intent is to catch myself before getting on a roll. While I may not mean to grumble, too often I am oblivious to doing so. Complaining can become a mindless habit.

Frequency. Behavior psychologists use something called a frequency count. A period of observation, say sixty minutes, is divided into smaller periods, say sixty seconds. The behavior of interest is counted in each period to get a better picture of its frequency.

To illustrate, little Butkus is disruptive in class. What exactly does "disruptive" mean? To be counted, it must first be defined: leaves his seat; talks out; bothers a classmate. A frequency count tallies the occurrence of each behavior, when it happens, and what percentage of the time it happens. It provides specifics.

What might be your complaint count? What are the numbers? Infrequent or recurrent? More frequent with your spouse, kids, father-in-law? What percentage of your conversations?

Another option: Ask a trusted someone — spouse, parent, child, friend — to be a behavior psychologist. Can she be objective and honest with you? You're seeking particulars: Do I complain? About what? How often? Is my percentage rising?

Person. The amount of complaining is often tied to who is listening. Some people hear more than their fair share about our life dissatisfactions, because we feel safe with them or because we know they'll listen for a long time, or because they have similar troubles. The saying is: Misery loves company. Of course, that doesn't mean the company wants to hear my misery.

As I write this, I'm as old as I've ever been. Pictures no longer do me justice; they look too much like me. With aging, even aging well, can come aches and maladies. These can foster a conversational litany, an organ recital, if you will. Here again I need to remind myself to look through the broader lens: I've lived long enough to have a litany. This should be my silent mantra, when I remember.

Is there someone who habitually lays his woes upon you, to seek not guidance or understanding but commiseration? Is your sense of sympathy stretched to its limit? What is your reaction: stare blankly, study your shoelaces, head to a bathroom, check caller ID before answering? Drawn out discontentedness can move the most patient person to retreat. Complaining eventually loses its audience.

A multi-country survey asked citizens to rate their life satisfaction. Impoverished countries were toward the top. The U.S. was toward the bottom. How is this? By most measures of comfort — shelter, material, financial, leisure — our existence surpasses theirs. Therein lies an answer. Because we live with these comforts (and blessings), we easily come to expect them. The temptation is to want heaven on earth. When life isn't heaven, the conditions are set for grumbling.

Is grumbling a sin? In itself, not typically. Even repeated grumbling may not be. It can, however, reveal an attitude of ingratitude. The rehearsal of displeasures, dislikes, dissatisfactions can sour one's demeanor.

The appetite for griping can always find food to feed it. Earth may not be heaven, but it is still God's gift. The more I complain, the more I'm telling God I don't appreciate His gifts.

7

I'm Good, I Say

Conduct an Internet search: "Self-esteem and children." You'll receive tens of millions of results. It's hard evidence that in a few decades, self-esteem has leaped from academic theories to the center of the cultural mind. It now leads the list of psychological virtues. The once-esteemed virtues, such as humility or meekness, have faded. Newer, more "enlightened" ideas of what makes a healthy psyche have pushed them aside.

Academic success, achievements, satisfying relationships, inner peace—all sorts of benefits purportedly accompany a strong self-image. Likewise, personal distress—self-doubt, inner conflict, unhappiness—goes up as self-esteem goes down.

Early on, children are taught the prescribed mantras. "You can't like others if you don't like yourself." (Really?) "I'm special." (If everybody is special, nobody is special.) "I'm always a winner." (Trophies and stickers for all.)

Reality is the judge of every "new and improved" notion of well-being. The self-esteem movement has been tested by reality and found wanting. Most of its predictions have unraveled in the face of closer scrutiny. At the risk of demeaning self-esteem, it really isn't related to any particular outcomes at all. And pursuing it for its own sake leads to self-centeredness.

Some years ago, a survey presented a list of high-profile people and asked, "How likely are these people to go to heaven?" Oprah Winfrey gained the second-most votes, with 66 percent of respondents believing she was heaven bound. Only Mother Teresa, at 79 percent, topped her. When asked, "How likely are *you* to go to heaven?", 87 percent of the respondents said they thought they were on their way. Most people, it turns out, rate themselves to be as holy, or even more so, than Mother Teresa.

At one level, Christians would agree with honestly valuing oneself. Every person has worth, inherent and infinite, not because we say so, but because every person is made in God's image. Real, lasting self-esteem comes from a divine declaration, not a human one.

"I'm a good person." Who defines "good"? If I do, why wouldn't I be in Mother Teresa's saintly league? I'm the judge of my own virtue. I set the moral bar, one I can reach even if I'm living badly. What's more, if I wish, I can slide the bar down to match my conduct. My standards, in the modern view of things, are as credible as God's.

Am I good by society's bar? After all, I don't lie, cheat, or steal (not regularly anyway). I'm a decent parent and spouse. I obey most laws, pay my taxes, and mostly mind my own business. My behavior is pretty much in line with what others and the law say is acceptable.

Society and the law, however, follow ever-shifting standards, which may or may not reflect God's never-shifting ones. Abortion is legal and approved by about half the population. Does that make it a moral good? Premarital sex, out-of-wedlock pregnancies, and even adultery have moved further into moral OK-ness in our culture. Are they no longer sins (gasp!) that can taint one's overall status as a good person? To quote Archbishop Fulton Sheen,

"Wrong is wrong even if everybody is wrong. Right is right even if nobody is right."

"I'm a good person" often leaves unsaid, "relatively speaking." If I do less bad than others, then, so the theory goes, I am more good. Given what others are doing or what I could be doing, I think I compare pretty well. God should be grateful.

If God declared goodness as we humans do, we'd all stand on solid spiritual ground. Instead, He has declared we all are sinners in need of His salvation, mercy, and grace. He isn't saying that we're all bad people; quite the contrary, He has also declared, "And God saw everything that he had made, and behold, it was very good" (Gen. 1:31). He has declared us to be infinitely valuable souls. That's the true basis of self-esteem.

My fallen human nature wraps me in my own self-interest. It's that self-interest that clouds my judgment of my own moral status. It serves me well to think well of me.

Jesus wouldn't be persuaded by the modern self-esteem movement. When instructing His followers about seeking accolades for doing good, He told them to consider themselves "unworthy servants," doing only what they should (Luke 17:10). In the eyes of experts, not very psychologically affirming.

Once again, the final word comes again from our Lord. When addressed as, "Good Teacher," he answered, "Why do you call me good? No one is good but God alone" (Mark 10:17–18).

8

Normal or Right?

There is one question I am asked more than any other. It speaks of uneasiness about one's psychological state. It speaks of a desire to be typical. And it speaks of the triumph of modern psychological principles over traditional morals.

That question is: Is it normal?

- My four-year-old melts down when he doesn't get his way. Is that normal for his age? He hit me last week. How much should I be concerned about that?
- My husband comes home from work in a bad mood at least twice a week. Do most people do that?
- My teenage son's room looks like a landfill. My friends tell me that's his age. All their kids' rooms look that way. But I'm just not sure.
- I seem to get upset over the littlest things. Am I losing it?

Is this typical? What does it mean? Should I be concerned? Is this just a phase? Does it reveal something deeper? The words vary, but the worry is the same: Is it normal?

The question is not easy to answer. Even those who make a living answering it — the mental-health professionals — regularly don't agree. In part, because the boundary between normal and not is fuzzy and fluid. How far out of the "norm" do actions have to be to be called abnormal or to get a psychological diagnosis?

Butkus averages three temper eruptions per week. Is that too many for a five-year-old? How about for an eleven-year-old? Are seven per week too may? How about twelve? He doesn't throw anything; he just cries. How long is too long? How loud is too loud? He runs to his room for ten minutes afterward. Is that OK? What about two hours? What about door slamming?

See the puzzle? How often, how loud, how long, how intense, how many? So many questions are related to the overall question: Is it normal?

It's a judgment call. Suppose 82 of 100 experts would agree, "That's not normal." What then? Whether Butkus throws one fit every four days or four every day, the behavior still has to be dealt with. Whether I lose my temper once a week or once a day, I still need to control myself better. If I want to love more like Christ, whether my behavior is "normal" by the world's standards is for the most part irrelevant. I have to act better however I can and through whatever help I can seek.

Numbers may indicate what is common. They are a poor measure of how best to live. More young adults under age thirty-five live together than choose marriage. Living together is now socially normal. About 3 percent of people enter marriage chaste. That means 97 percent don't. They are the norm, overwhelmingly so. One survey indicated that approximately 90 percent of eleven- to nineteen-year-olds have seen Internet pornography, intentionally or accidentally. Most teens have televisions in their bedrooms. Those who don't are in a shrinking minority.

What is the norm or typical is often something to resist. Consider the wife who is very unhappy in her marriage. Everyone she tells advises her to leave, abandon the union, seek happiness elsewhere. Were she to conduct a poll, most would advise, "End the marriage." Persevering is not the accepted course. Indeed, by the numbers, it's thought foolish.

A relative is hostile to your faith and moral beliefs. The slights are predictable and regular. How would most people react? Avoid? Agree? Assail? Instead, you smile, shrug, or shift the conversation. Some, maybe most, would see you as naïve, a doormat, weakly passive. Should you imitate the standard responses of the crowd?

"After all she's done to me, I think it's very normal to want to retaliate." "I have every right to tell him exactly what I think." "Anybody having to listen to his nonsense would do exactly as I did." We tell ourselves, in effect: How I act, however badly, is normal and, by extension, all right.

I will ask parents, "Do you want to raise a child whose character reflects his peers or a child of exceptional character?" None yet has answered that common character is their goal. All want a child-become-adult of uncommon character. They want him to be abnormal—in the healthiest sense.

"Is it normal?" supersedes a far more critical question: Is it right or good? It is typical, yes, for a three-year-old to emotionally erupt. It's not good, and it needs to be disciplined away. As a rule, children get more lippy as they move into adolescence. Is disrespect at *that age* developmentally all right?

I can always claim others would act as poorly as I would, given my circumstances. The "to be expected" nature of my conduct does not make it good or right. Something can be ever so common and still be shameful. Think sin.

"It's normal" can be a justification for avoiding self-scrutiny. If I'm convinced that my poor behavior is the default response of most people, the more important question, "How should *I* personally act?" won't be asked—much less answered.

Thinking Like Jesus

To once again quote Archbishop Fulton Sheen: "Wrong is wrong even if everybody is wrong. Right is right even if nobody is right." And normal doesn't mean right.

9

It Passes — Fast

If I could rewrite my life, one of the first chapters I'd edit would be those times I hurled harsh words from out of raw emotion. I would put all those I love, along with those I labor to love, into one long paragraph and write, "I'm sorry. I take it back." Whatever I thought I'd win by some peevish or scorching words, I later lost tenfold in remorse, regret, or seeing another's welling anger or hurt. It's universal: The impulse to speak too quickly is always lurking. In an instant, the heart rules the head, with damaging repercussions.

My rough estimate is that 82.617 percent of my uglier words accompany my first surge of upset feelings. I suppose I could fall back on the excuse that I was too emotional to stop myself, but that wouldn't really be so. Rarely does anyone reach the point of zero self-control.

The remnants of a heated exchange can cook up a stew, the mental rehearsal over and over again of the unpleasant point-counterpoint. It's the lingering desire to speak one's peace. (Now there's a misnomer.)

Fortunately, time intrudes. It allows cooler thoughts to quench fiery emotions. Better judgment cautions one to leave unsaid what else could have been said.

At peak emotion, however, judgment is impaired. When one is feeling accused, put down, or hurt, mind and body react in tandem. The mind says, "Defend yourself. Don't let him get away with that." The body says, "Here's a rush of emotion to get you started."

Once again, time is an ally. If you can say nothing for the briefest part of a minute, the urge to say anything will pass—rapidly. The words in your head fighting for voice will lose momentum. Mouth control here is more than mental. It is also physical. The just-released flood of chemicals will start to taper, their effect relatively short-lived. (I know, it doesn't feel so. An example of "time is relative.") It's a physiological fact: The longer you stay quiet, the easier (less hard?) it will be to stay quiet.

Strength training provides a parallel: Longtime weight lifters may reach a bench press of over three hundred pounds. To the novice, pushing that amount of metal against gravity is inconceivable. He must first find a weight his muscles can manage. With perseverance, his numbers will increase. What was once too heavy becomes doable.

Holding back your tongue, which weighs four ounces, during heavy emotions, might seem comparable to bench-pressing your own weight your first day at the gym. With practice, you can do both. Holding your tongue is the more worthwhile and rewarding exercise.

St. James says, "Though [ships] are so great and are driven by strong winds, they are guided by a very small rudder wherever the will of the pilot directs. So the tongue is a little member and . . . is a fire" (James 3:4-6).

Not every fiery situation makes you bench-press your own weight. Master first those instants that don't require Herculean effort. Mouth control builds with repetition. What was once hard will later take less discipline.

Can't ugly thoughts be as bad as ugly words? That depends. How long do they linger? Are you inviting them in to fester? Are they a rehash of the missed opportunity to say what you could have said? Or, did they flare instantly, a cerebral knee-jerk? "Why would he say that? Who is she to correct me? I didn't ask for his opinion."

Pushing away ugly thoughts is akin to pushing away tempta-tion. The urge arrives; the will conquers it. Hurtful words can flash into the mind at the speed of thought. Giving them voice does the damage.

"I'm just speaking my mind." Am I speaking my mind, or my emotions? Speaking my mind implies speaking my thinking. Speak-ing my emotions may feel like what I'm thinking. All too often, away from the intensity of the moment, it isn't what I think at all.

Suppose my wife has asked me several times to fix her dresser drawer, which is jammed in its track. I have every intention of do-ing so. Why is she reminding me every month? One Sunday morn-ing before Mass, after wrestling with the drawer, she says, "Maybe you won't fix this because it doesn't affect you." Thoughtlessly, I retaliate, "Maybe your parents raised a princess who wants what she wants done yesterday." Ouch. Is that what I think? Not even close. Is it what I said? Can't dispute that. Two kids also heard me. My reflex emotion led to reflex words — completely untrue ones. Hope-fully, I will retract and correct them before we walk into church.

"I just needed to vent." Some older theories agree. They de-clared that choking back emotions pressing for release is unhealthy, both to the body and the psyche. They need a vocal outlet, an exit for the steam. Newer studies have taken a different view. Control-ling one's immediate emotions is often the healthier course. Rather than purging boiling emotions, venting can actually fuel them.

Consider rain falling on saturated ground. It carves its own little channels, running deeper and faster with more water. It seeks the dirt path of least resistance.

Thinking Like Jesus

Rough words are like rainwater. The quicker they flow this time around, the easier they flow next time around. They become a response of first resort. Venting becomes freer with each vent.

"Some things need to be said." Perhaps they do. Timing, again, is relevant. Almost always, wisdom says to delay. More settled emotions lead to more settled thoughts. The rush to say all you once thought needed to be said may moderate. Calm is more clear and credible.

A military chaplain told me that his instinct used to be to jump on his computer to express his grievance toward someone. Only a few such e-mails taught him: Store them as drafts for a day. Most were later sent to the trash. As he puts it, "Send is not your friend."

It's worth repeating: When you most feel like saying harsh words, don't say them. What initially felt like overpowering emotions will weaken quicker than you think. With time, you'll need less strength of will to remain quiet.

You never have to apologize for what you didn't say. Catholics know, too: You never have to confess what you didn't say.

10

The Authentic Self

"Self" is a highly regarded word in the lexicon of psychologists—self-image, self-esteem, self-meaning, self-pursuit, self-actualization. This is understandable, as the world of psychology is predominately the world of the individual. The focus on the self has birthed a number of fashionable self-proclamations.

"I've got to be me." It makes for a popular song title, but it makes little sense. If I, generally soft-spoken, verbally blister my father-in-law for something he says, who does the assaulting? Is it not me? It may not be consistent with my overall demeanor, but at the time and place, *it is me*. It had to be me.

A father abandons his wife and children for an online tryst. That may not be "who he was" up until the Internet contact. It is now. "But that is so unlike him." No, *it is like him* under the present circumstances.

"I've got to be me." Does this mean I will act according to my feelings or desires? If so, I'm acting mindlessly. My urge to smack an irritable someone may be nearly overwhelming, but I'm smart—also more Christlike—to resist it. Am I me or not me by keeping my hand to myself? Who is the real me?

"The authentic self." That would make for a good self-help book title, if it isn't one already. Pursuing personal wholeness, according to some theories, involves pursuing one's "authentic self," uncovering the "me" at my uncompromising core. It's a psychologically chic way of saying, "What you see is who I am."

What if the image ain't pretty? The authentic self may not be the better part of me. With God's help, I strive to slowly alter the "real" self. To be ruled by my genuine self may allow too much of my ugly self to emerge: anger, lust, greed, envy, sloth, as well as self-promotion, self-centeredness, self-absorption.

"There are no masks in my personality." Meaning: I tell you what I think and feel, whenever and however? (A very off-putting style.) Meaning: I tell it like it is? (Or like *you think* it is.) Meaning: You'll always get the unmasked me? (But the masked me might be a nicer sight.)

I wear an "I like you" countenance around an uncle I struggle to like. I put on a smiley face at a family gathering I'm enjoying as much as an IRS audit. I look serene, but my insides are churning. Wearing a mask is not always phony or deceptive. Often it is the better way to live. Who knows: Wear the mask long enough, and it may transform the face underneath for the better.

"That's not who I am." In marriage counseling I might advise a spouse to show more affection, as his spouse is craving the slightest morsel of it. But he sees himself as an unemotional, unexpressive person. In his mind, being more affectionate is acting against his persona.

A mother would enjoy her son more if she were a firmer disciplinarian. She sees herself as a "soft, caring" parent and changing now, she says, would run counter to her nature, one which she favors. A daughter-in-law could enhance family peace by arguing less with her husband's mother but is reluctant because "I'm an assertive person."

The Authentic Self

"That's not who I am" is a far-reaching justification for living as one wishes. It's a defense against self-improvement, to co-opt another "self" word. It undercuts loving another more than oneself.

"That's not who I am" speaks to a false sense of self. It says, "I can't change" or, rather, "I won't change." "That's not me" may sound psychologically grown-up, but it's Christian childhood.

"That's not who I am" has a variant: "I've never done that before." From birth forward, every single thing we do begins as a "never before." The most long-standing virtue was once a first-time act.

"I've never done this before" can mean a number of things. First: The activity is novel, but it's not a contradiction of my personality. I've never written a book, played chess, changed a diaper, cliff dived, and so on. Second, it *is* a contradiction to my personality. My prevailing inclination is so ingrained that it would seriously interfere with my behaving otherwise.

Third, this conduct is out of character for me. It's not my way. Meaning three is most relevant here. When I've never done something that I know would be good to do, I can settle deeper into inertia. That is, I can get more comfortable and satisfied with inaction.

An example for fathers: Suppose you would rather cliff dive than leap into a swirling mother-child verbal maelstrom. In the past, only hurricane volume made you jump.

In this particular episode, however, you're determined to support your wife. No more sitting idly by waiting for the storm to pass. Rising from the couch, you head straight toward your daughter. "She's not only Mom that you're talking to like that. She's my wife. Go to your room. She and I are going to decide what to do about this."

Your wife may wonder, "Who are you? What have you done with my husband?" Even your daughter may not know what to think, especially if listening from a distance has always been your preferred approach, or, as it were, non-approach. She's come to interpret your inaction as tacit approval of her action. Are you switching sides?

No matter who thinks what, your first-time immersion will be the first time only once. Every succeeding time that you protect your wife will accumulate into a new pattern, one very salutary to your marriage. Repetition is how the never-before becomes routine.

Sir Isaac Newton discovered the scientific law of inertia. In part it states, "A body at rest will remain at rest unless acted upon by an outside force." A parallel to human beings is: A body (in this case, mine) will remain at rest (not seeking virtue) unless acted upon by an inside force (my will and God's grace).

With every repeat, a never-before behavior gains momentum. It becomes a pattern that becomes a style that becomes a personality.

"I've got to be me" is true all the time for all of us. I am the "me" who is capable of acting inconsistently, unpredictably, "out of character." Christians recognize this as fallen human nature. The guiding self-concept for Christians should be "I've got to be *a better me*."

11

Unmet Needs

Abraham Maslow was a high-profile professor during the early days of psychology. His ideas about personality competed with others at a time when constructing all-encompassing theories of the human condition was in vogue.

Maslow proposed that people were motivated according to a "hierarchy of needs." At the bottom are the most basic — air, water, food, safety; the stuff of survival. One level up are the psychological — love, belonging, accomplishment. At the peak of the pyramid is "self-actualization" — the need to achieve one's full potential. Maslow maintained that individuals climbed higher as each lower need was satisfied.

Over time, psychology recognized the impossibility of compacting all the complexities of being human into a one-size-fits-all theory. Nonetheless, remnants of past attempts reverberate into the present. And the language of "needs" is a prime remnant.

"I just don't feel my needs are being met." "He doesn't consider my needs." "I have needs, too." "She only thinks about her own needs."

What are these unmet needs? Not so much food, shelter, and protection, but social and emotional "needs" — understanding, communication, affection, respect. Almost anything I believe to be essential to my contentment as a spouse, parent, or friend, I can deem a "need."

A definition of need: a lack of something deemed necessary. By this definition, *true needs* reside at the bottom of Maslow's hierarchy—air, water, food, shelter. Much of what Maslow, along with the modern therapeutic lexicon, calls "needs" are more accurately called "desires." Other words are "preferences" or "wants." Giving something the status of a "need" primes us for resentment should it go unfulfilled. The relationship: The stronger my demand for something, the stronger my indignation when my demand isn't met.

It's a small step from a need to an entitlement. I *need* your respect; I *need* your cooperation; I *need* you to quit judging me; I *need* understanding. Translation: You aren't treating me as you should. Not "as I want to be treated" or "as I'd like to be treated," but as it's *my right* to be treated. And if I'm not so treated, I feel cheated.

For a Christian, the problem in such thinking is that we are called to be less mindful of our "needs" and more mindful of others', whether those needs are for food or for understanding. Truly a calling that runs counter to our deep inclinations.

Isn't love and its companions—respect, care, affection, kindness, mercy—critical for human well-being? To be sure. Peak well-being, however, comes from *showing* these qualities rather than *being shown* them. A focus on my self-defined needs keeps my eyes trained on me.

A popular relationship program has coined the term "Love Languages." It proposes that spouses give and receive love through preferred forms of expression, or "languages." These are time, touch, affirmation, service, and gifts. I might want my wife to show me more affection—the language of touch. She, on the other hand, wishes I'd be more available to her and the kids—the language of time. Each of us speaks and hears love in individual ways.

Unmet Needs

As a Christian spouse, I can't fall back on, "Hey, I mow the lawn," knowing she'd really like to hear "I love you" now and then. I owe it to her to speak the language she best understands. On the other hand, while I might desire more affection from her, if I don't get it, I can't think, "If you don't love me how I *need*, then how you do love me doesn't mean as much." I love her best when I speak her language. I can't demand she speak mine.

"Need talk" is a verbal quagmire for a Christian. It inclines one to feel emotionally shortchanged or relationally deprived. Wanting better treatment from another is understandable. The temptation to elevate wants into requirements, however, is ever present. Too much talk of "my needs" doesn't befit a follower of Christ.

12

Change Them

How many psychologists does it take to change a light bulb? Only one, but the light bulb has to really want to be changed.

That old joke illuminates an unchanging law of therapy: No matter how competent the therapist, the client has to cooperate. He has to want to change.

Talk therapy has an esteemed reputation in the cultural mind. Despite that, its rate of success—as measured by real, positive change—is rather disappointing, and some would say dismal. Why? The reasons are nearly as diverse as the clients: expecting therapy to be "magic"; a limited sense of personal responsibility; the passing of the initial "crisis"; scheduling complications; finances. And last but not least: having little or no desire to change.

Therapy would seem to be a prime channel for change. The client acknowledges the expertise and experience of the therapist. He recognizes that something—or some things—have gone awry. And he's willing to pay for help. Why, then, does positive change not happen as often as one might think? The answer lies at the heart of the human condition: Self-improvement is a slow, lifelong process—assuming one even sees the value in it.

Thinking Like Jesus

To sustain my professional enthusiasm and energy, early on I had to accept the reality that I could help some people and not others. Had my youthful confidence not been adjusted to meet reality, "burnout" would have long ago caught up to me. And I'd be writing books instead of doing therapy. Oh, wait …

Whether in counseling or in appeals from friends and family, I hear one thing routinely: Tell me how to change another person.

The answer combines good and bad news. The good: How we relate and react to another can change his behavior sometimes for better, sometimes for worse. To repeat a theme of this book: The path to changing another runs through changing oneself.

The bad: Changing ourselves for the better may not change another. No matter how loving, how reasonable, how persevering, how forgiving we are, if another person sees no reason to change herself, she's not going to.

Understandably, the hope lives on that through proper preaching, reasonable reassuring, and endless entreaties, another will come to see some light. Something deep within us wants to believe we can reach anyone, if only we can find the key. The fact that, for now anyway, he might remain locked, no matter what keys we have, is hard to accept. It seems like a surrender, a giving up of hope. (Prayer, though, can always continue.) One piece of advice, then: Don't be a therapist.

It is not a surrender of hope to acknowledge human free will. Who knew human nature better than Christ? Who was a better psychologist? Who was more reasonable, wise, forgiving? Did He change the hearts and minds of the religious leaders? Despite our Lord's infinite knowledge, He ran into human stubbornness. Are we better able than Christ to bend someone's will?

Parents whose adult children have rejected or drifted from the Faith are often desperate to reach them with the truth in which they were raised. They want to find some prescription to change their hearts, to put them back on the path toward God. When they can't, they despair, or push the kids even further from themselves and God by not letting the matter rest.

A major source of distress is often the obstinate reality that another's behavior shows no sign of changing—a spouse, grown child, parent, family member, friend, religious leader. At some point, for one's own peace and for the sake of the relationship, one has to release the desire, or the demand, that the other be different than he is or has been for years, even decades.

Why would someone not want to change for the better? First, she doesn't see the same reasons for her to change as you do. In fact, she doesn't see any problem with who she is at all. Second, she may have some insight into the problem, but not enough to push her through the hard emotional work involved in self-scrutiny and self-improvement. Third, what you see as a problem isn't one. Your perception needs to change. That is, you may think she needs to make some key personality or life changes, but it could be just your opinion. As most always, the place to look first is toward oneself, asking, "Do *I* need to change the way *I* look at this person?"

A college graduate chooses to work as a server in a local restaurant, supporting himself independently. Dad pushes him to work within his degree field, wanting him to change his job choice. Is the son doing anything wrong, or is he just behaving in a way his dad wouldn't?

A daughter is raising her children more loosely than Grandma raised her. Grandma believes daughter needs to "fix" her parenting style. Does daughter have the right to parent as she sees fit? Is this a case of needed change, or Grandma-wanted change?

I may want others to be different because they aren't thinking or acting as I would. They are not acting wrongly or hurtfully. They are acting in their own ways, different from mine.

Thinking Like Jesus

"Aren't I obliged to help someone see their sin? Can't I be held morally responsible if I don't?" For one, those closest to us know where we stand morally. We raised them; we live with them; we've talked to them. Do we keep repeating what they already know from us?

For another, vigilance for opportunities to raise the subject again and again can strain your relationship. Conversations become stiff when one or more parties anticipate the same touchy subject lurking just around the next sentence. Remove the verbal risk, and you'll remove some two-way uneasiness.

The religious leaders of our Lord's day censured Him because He ate with tax collectors, who were considered among the most despicable of sinners. Dining at the same table wasn't seen as a nice, social get-together; it meant deep fellowship. Scripture nowhere records Jesus saying, "OK, guys, don't think any of this means I approve of your conduct. And you've got two weeks to resign, or you won't be talking with me anymore." No, the sinners and everybody else (except perhaps the religious leaders who demanded He change) knew where Jesus stood. Nonetheless, He continued to reach out to them.

A simple prayer popularly known as the Serenity Prayer entreats: God, grant me the serenity to accept the things I cannot change, courage to change the things I can, and wisdom to know the difference.

Substitute "people" for "things" and you've got a good guiding prayer for easing your personal distress. You'll also go a long way to easing what you were convinced were destined to be distressing relationships.

13

Toxic People

Counselors are quick to counsel: Avoid those who disturb your peace. In therapeutic lingo: Avoid those "toxic" to your well-being. Maximum emotional health depends on minimizing, even eliminating, contact with such personal afflictions.

"I'm happier if I stay away from my brother." "My anxiety skyrockets when I'm around my mother-in-law." "My daughter and her husband can upset me more than anyone else, so I make excuses not to see them."

Note who's not in the circle of toxicity: a surly neighbor, a self-righteous second cousin, an overbearing little-league coach. Why not? You see the neighbor from your car as you pass his house, the second cousin only on Christmas Eve, and the coach twice a season when playing his team. Contact with them is minimal. So is any emotional toll.

Not so with family, close relations, and adult children. (Adolescents can multiply your stress, but they can't yet afford their own apartment.) These are our inner circle, those most able, for better or worse, to arouse in us the most intense emotions. They are also those, except in the extreme, we shouldn't avoid. We are obliged as Christians to get along with them—or, at a minimum, tolerate them however possible.

When a counselee says that a family member so stresses her that she thinks it's best to shun him, I ask, "Are you playing any part in your stress?" At that, I get a "What's that mean?" look. "Well, since the stressing person isn't in my office, I can only help the one who *is*: you. Is there a part of your stress, even if small, that is self-induced?" Reducing it can move a relationship from "toxic" to unpleasant, and perhaps to bearable. All the more worthwhile when family peace is at stake.

"He disturbs my peace" is better translated, "I disturb my peace about him." Is this semantics, a bit of psycho-speak? On the contrary, it's just accurate. How we react to others makes us more or less willing to associate with them. Questions to ask yourself are: How much am I allowing this person to upset me? Am I giving her opinions too much credibility? Do I project onto him intent that isn't there? Am I taking her words personally when they are coming from her own insecurity? Am I expecting him to act any differently than he always has? Right answers aren't so critical when the person involved is the neighbor three doors down. They are when the person is your mother.

Suppose you find your mother opinionated, disagreeable, critical, or some other combination of personality pejoratives. Survey twenty people who know her, and seventeen of them will agree with you. Would this be reason to slide from, "Most other people think she's hard to take" to "I want her out of my life"? For emotional reasons, it could seem so. For Christian reasons, likely not.

"I would feel so much better if we didn't have contact." No doubt. Certain people seem to have the capacity to step all over our most sensitive spots. Still, are uncomfortable, even very uncomfortable, feelings reason to label those people "toxic" and determine to purge the "poison"?

It's a relationship truth: We are able to get along with so-called toxic people better than we think. Sometimes that simply means getting along with them less poorly—ignoring slights, keeping quiet, forgetting offenses more than two years old. We may not want to. We may think the energy needed to keep the connection civil isn't worth it. It is, though, when that person's life intersects with ours, whether we like it or not.

Couldn't some relationships be considered truly toxic? Aren't there those who are so hostile, abusive, or unpredictable that contact with them jeopardizes oneself or one's loved ones? Yes. Fortunately, this extreme doesn't intrude in most people's lives. Terms such as "abusive," "hostile," and "unpredictable" are often applied when "difficult" would be more fitting. If the difficult one is a parent, we still are commanded to honor him. We aren't commanded to obey his every dictate or to enjoy being around him. We are commanded to give him the respect that is his God-ordained due.

Similarly, we aren't obliged to support or enable an irresponsible, uncooperative adult child. We can, if possible, try to keep some sort of connection with him, however fragile.

"How I act around [Name] makes her a near occasion of sin for me." Living by this logic would rapidly shrink one's social circle. Many sins are born during person-to-person contact. As the familiar saw says, "I love mankind; it's the people who give me trouble." Unless someone *directly* pushes me to sin, I am responsible for my conduct around him. It would be more accurate to say, "I am my own near occasion of sin in his presence."

Parents wistfully reminisce about being less "sinful" pre-children. Prior to living in the same house with kids, they saw themselves as calmer, more easygoing, less childish. A common lament: "My son and I butt heads; it's because we're too much alike." Who is on whose level? Am I pulling him up to mine, or is he pulling me down to his? Childrearing impatience is routinely one of the first things out of a parent's mouth in confession. Does that make the child a near occasion of sin? If we talk to him more harshly than we talk to any adults, could he rightly think *us* "toxic"?

Few people are so disturbing as to need to be erased from one's life. Calling someone "toxic" is a call to look at oneself. Do I have room to improve *myself* when around him? If so, while I still might not like being around him, I will no longer think my best option is not to be around him.

14

Value-Laden Words Are Bad

"For God so loved the world that he gave his only Son, that whoever believes in him should not perish but have eternal life" (John 3:16).

An evangelical preacher commented with some chagrin that John 3:16 is no longer the Bible verse he hears quoted most frequently. Another has replaced it: "Judge not, that you be not judged" (Matt. 7:1).

No surprise, as this reflects a fast-spreading cultural mindset: "Don't tell me what I do is wrong. Who are you to judge me?" Christ is quoted as an ally even by those who don't like much of the rest of what He said.

Christians know what Christ really meant: We are in no position to judge *the state of another's soul.* That is God's call. Our call is to know God's standards for what is right and what is wrong. *That* is what we judge.

Ironically, as fewer kinds of conduct are called sinful, a new sin has arisen: judgment. Everyday language confirms this attitude—language with roots in the mental-health lexicon.

In graduate school, I was taught a second language. Call it the language of non-judgmentalism. It sounds like this:

"Angela, pushing Conan is unacceptable."

"Don't you think jumping on my computer is an unfortunate decision, Cliff?"

"Rob, stealing is a poor choice."

"We don't ride our bike through the flowers, Harley. It's inappropriate." (What's with "we"? It's been weeks since I've ridden my bike through the flowers.)

Politicians, too, have adopted the lingo. "I'm sorry; I was wrong," has been replaced with: "Mistakes were made." I wouldn't want to begin confession with, "Bless me, Father, my choices were misguided."

The new, value-stripped language has replaced outdated, guilt-inducing throwbacks such as "wrong" and "bad." According to many experts, no one should be made to feel guilt, or its vile cousin, shame. These things are bad—I mean, *unfortunate*.

Using morally neutral words, so the thinking goes, is a reminder to shun "unhealthy" moral scrutiny that might hurt one's "self-esteem." "Unacceptable" or "inappropriate" sends no message of judgment; instead it says, "At this time and place, it would have been more appropriate to act otherwise." The context of the behavior is what makes it undesirable, not so much the behavior itself.

Can we call any behavior wrong? Kicking a puppy? Biting your sister? Rooting for the New York Yankees if you live in Boston? Is a husband who, seeking his own pleasure, abandons his wife and three children acting only "inappropriately"? Or is he wrong, *very wrong* and are his choices bad, *very bad*?

Calling lying, cheating, stealing, and screaming at one's mother "unacceptable" or "impermissible" trivializes their moral status. Growing in virtue, whether as a child or adult, involves a clear sense of right and wrong, good and evil, moral and immoral. Value-neutral language closes the distance between these poles of human conduct and serves only to blur healthy judgment. Experts might be averse to using these terms, but most people instinctively understand they are essential guides to right conduct.

The movement toward nonjudgmental talk has pulled in parents. Out of fear that morally "insensitive" words will hurt their children's self-image, they carefully qualify their discipline:

"You are good, but your behavior is not."

"I like you; I don't like what you did."

"Your conduct is unpleasant; you're not."

Though well-meant, such distinctions are generally too subtle for children, especially younger ones. Separating actions from self takes sophisticated reasoning. Sherlock's elementary conclusion is, "I acted bad, so I am bad."

To differentiate "Who I am" from "What I do" is an exercise for the smartest of philosophers. Nonetheless, parents are cautious to reinforce, "I'm not judging *you*." They remind little Justice that they're talking about his conduct and not his person. The reminders may help, but the real lesson of love lies in parents' *actions*. Through their unconditional love, shown in everyday actions, their child does come to understand that calling his behavior bad or wrong is in no way a personal put-down.

Conscience is a casualty of the value-neutral language movement. Christians afford conscience an exalted status, deservedly so. A well-formed conscience is a crucial warning bell that says, "What I'm doing is wrong. I know it, not just intellectually, but in my spirit." The conscience serves as a governor on desires and passions. It provokes post-sin feelings—guilt, shame, embarrassment—that can be spiritually fruitful, but that are also the very feelings some theories now proclaim to be neurotic remnants of another, more morally stifling time.

Granted, conscience can also torment. Some people are shackled by a false sense of chronic sinning. They "feel" unworthy of God's love. (Who is worthy?) An intrusive, relentless conscience convicts them. The name given to this is scrupulosity, a depressing sense of never being right with God. It does not result from a healthy conscience, but from one run amok.

A healthy conscience doesn't shun words like "bad" or "wrong." It uses them to the soul's benefit. Like the child who hears repeatedly that Mom loves him no matter how he acts, the Christian knows that no matter how he acts, God always loves him and stands ever ready to accept his repentance.

A follower of Christ welcomes value-laden words into his vocabulary. They are sure guides to living within God-revealed morals. If God says something is good, it is. If He says something is wrong, it is. The Bible nowhere uses the language of moral neutrality.

If centuries of experience are any guide, it is not the presence of moral words that damages the psyche. It is their absence.

15

A Generic Sinner

Some years ago I spoke at a conference on morality. Two present-ers spoke before me. Both told of their lives prior to knowing Christ — lives jam-packed with sordid immorality, turbulence, and looming self-destruction. They emphasized not only the spiritual salvation they found upon conversion, but the salvation of their everyday lives as well. The contrast between the darkness of their pre-Christian days and the light of their post-conversion ones was dramatic and moving.

Tongue planted firmly in cheek, I began my presentation. "I'm not sure I belong here. I have no heathen-to-Christ life story. I grew up in a loving two-parent home where the Catholic Faith was taught and practiced. I never passed through a self-ruinous phase from which Christ rescued me. I hope I still have something to offer you."

Despite the radical contrast in our stories, one fundamental similarity connected us: Then and now, they and I are sinners. Our natures are bent toward selfish desires and self-interest. No matter how much God shapes us, our inclination toward sin remains until we are in His presence.

Thinking Like Jesus

Psychologists talk of cognitive dissonance, which refers to holding two contradictory ideas in one's head simultaneously. Working to reconcile this contradiction can cause mental distress. Two such ideas for Christians are these: I am a sinner; and I am infinitely valuable. How can this be? By human reasoning alone, it doesn't add up. Of course, the answer lies not in our nature, but in God's. He loves us *as we are*, but, as the familiar saying goes, He loves us too much *to leave us as we are*.

Another pair of dissonant notions: I sin repeatedly; and each and every time, if penitent, I am forgiven, with no limit. Again, these two realities seem incompatible using only human reason. The discord created by these notions can lead to scrupulosity—an agonizing worry that one is too bad to be forgiven.

On one hand, I know by faith that God loves me no matter what. On the other, I know by experience that I would be pushed to my limit, and perhaps beyond, to forgive someone who sins against me as much as I sin against God.

Nonetheless, I accept the label "sinner." It is an unalterable truth, and everybody else wears the same label, whether they accept it or not. I've even grown more comfortable with the label—but only up to a point. I'm not comfortable wearing the label when it gets too specific. I can call myself a sinner, and you can confirm it—but just don't get too exact about it: "I notice that you tend to brag a lot about your kids." "You're late again. Why do you make people wait on you?" "You've got a bit of a temper, I see."

I marshal my defenses: "I don't think it's bragging. It's normal to be proud of your kids. Most parents are." "I'm not that late. I would have been here sooner, but I ran into some unexpected delays." "I'll admit, I got a little irritated this time around. But overall I think I stayed pretty cool."

Denial, defensiveness, downplaying—they all share a common theme: "I really didn't do anything wrong." While I do admit I'm capable of wrongdoing, I don't like my *individual wrongs* pointed out, however minor. That's getting a little too close to my sinfulness.

Couldn't someone accuse me of wrongdoing when none is present? Couldn't the charge come from his own insecurity, touchiness, intolerance, or misperception? Sure, and sorting out whether the problem is mine or his can take honest self-scrutiny. And that begins not with reflexively invalidating his point because it touches on a sin I don't want to recognize, but with examining my conscience.

Our Lord instructed us to remove the log from our eyes before reaching to remove the sliver from another's (Matt. 7:5). He warned that we are regularly blinded to our own faults, however major, while we remain acutely aware of others', however minor.

A study asked husbands and wives to write down their spouse's weaknesses. I suspect "Time's up!" had to be called out several times. Each spouse identified in exacting detail where and how the other needed to straighten up.

They were then instructed to write down their own shortcomings. The lists were noticeably shorter and tempered by self-tolerance. "Sometimes I could be more agreeable." "I don't always apologize when I should." The upshot: "We're both sinners, but I think you have the thicker catalogue."

My ears close fastest when I hear "trait" words—thoughtless, self-centered, critical, opinionated, judgmental, hot-tempered. It's safer to admit to an occasional slip-up than to a pattern. A negative *personality characteristic* is threatening to my view of myself. It makes me want to counter, "I'm not like that!" Of course, the trait "sinner" is about as broad as it gets, and I don't argue about being called that.

To better understand what you're being accused of, ask: What do I do to make you say (or feel, or do) that? How do I do that? Is this a habit for me? How did you take what I said? How often do you think this?

Your intent is to peek inside the other person's head, to get past his words and your first reaction. Don't reflexively explain or defend yourself. You are on a sin fact-finding mission. How did this person come to see you as he does?

Let us pray: "Jesus, help me see myself." And as long as it's Jesus who helps me, I'm open to correction. If it's Jesus working through someone else, well ...

Someone's observation may sound to you like raw nonsense, a double standard, or a complete misunderstanding. It's a challenge, but don't push to correct it. More often than not, an argument will commence. Instead, admit to whatever portion of the blame is yours.

The true test of humility: Thank him for his help. You'll probably shock him into silence. It's hard to continue criticizing someone who's not arguing with you.

I am a sinner. I admit it. It's too obvious to deny. What I don't want to admit are the particular sins that make me a sinner. I will walk closer to Christ, though, as I become more willing to admit what my sins are that earn me the rightful name "sinner."

16

Apology Averse

Christ is pretty clear on the subject: If you do something wrong, admit it, repent, and, if possible, make it right. If the wrong affects another person, go to him and seek forgiveness. "I'm sorry" is a good place to start.

Two small words, easy to pronounce. Loaded with healing, both for the speaker and the listener. They also rank as two of the hardest words to choke out in the English language.

During marriage counseling I will ask a spouse: When did you last apologize? "At our daughter's fourth birthday party." How old is your daughter? "She's a lawyer." Or: "At our wedding rehearsal dinner. I spilled some coffee on her lap and said, 'Sorry about that.'" Or: "How often does Halley's Comet swing by?"

The themes cluster: "I'm always the one to apologize; he thinks he's never wrong; she will never admit her fault; just once I'd like to hear, 'I'm sorry.'" Not uncommonly, these themes can emerge in marriages that claim to be Christ-centered.

What is it about "I'm sorry" that sticks in so many throats? No matter how needed and beneficial, the journey from the heart to the mouth still includes many obstacles: "My apology will be rejected; it will sound like I'm admitting to more than my share of blame; I shouldn't have to be the one to apologize; I'll be saying, 'I'm all wrong, you're all right.'" The top ranked hurdle: "I wasn't wrong."

Do you struggle to apologize, even when you believe you should? One theme runs through all those objections above: insecurity—that is, a delicate self-worth. The more delicate, the more reluctance to admit wrong, blame, or sin. Such confessions only further bruise the ego.

When self-worth is tied to "I'm sorry," the words mean too much: "I'm a failure" or "I'm inadequate" or "I'm a mess" or "I'm a jerk" or "I'm a sinner." (Shock!) They don't say, "I acted foolishly," but, "I'm foolish." They don't say, "I acted badly," but, "I'm a bad person." They don't say, "I shouldn't have done that," but, "I'm the kind of person who does that."

An apology only adds to my self-doubt—in faith, parenting, marriage, vocation.

In only a few decades the self-esteem movement has surged into the cultural psyche. Distilled to its essence, it says, "I am a wonderful person because I say so." Therein lies its core flaw. If Ray Guarendi asserts that Ray Guarendi is a wonderful human being, what is his evidence? His say-so. Am I the most unbiased person to make that judgment? The self-esteem movement—absent God—is a movement of self-declaration.

Christians' self-esteem comes from God. He declares us to be of infinite worth. (Non-Christians have the same worth; they just may not know it.) And God's declaration is unchangeable, independent of our good or bad conduct, and our worthy or unworthy apology.

If apologies come hard for you, realize: Your self-worth is not tied one bit to your "I'm sorry," no matter if it's rejected, misunderstood, or used against you. Your dignity has already been established. It's protected by God. You don't need to keep protecting it yourself.

By "risking" an apology, you are trusting in God's promise: You are my child. Your "I'm sorry" says, "Dear Lord, I rely on You to keep me focused on You, Who makes me truly valuable, with all my faults."

There is something I call the "Personal Apology Percentage" (PAP), which is one's perceived share of fault in any given argument or conflict. Absent a fault meter to provide an objective readout, my subjective judgment sets the number. Is it safe to say I'm not the most impartial observer? Further, my estimate of my own wrongdoing is usually a lowball.

Let's say that Jerkface—so labeled by a panel of observers—is judged to be 42 percent blameworthy during an edgy confrontation. Conversely, She-witch—again, the panel's label—started it, fueled it, and shouted it shut. Her fault percentage is assessed at 49. The two lay the last 9 percent on the kids. Both can legitimately claim, "It wasn't all my fault." In fact, neither one was even half at fault. Nonetheless, each has something to apologize for.

What's your PAP? In your mind, how much do you have to be wrong before acknowledging it? The ultimate goal is to apologize for your percentage, whatever that is. Maybe once you needed to be 51 perecent wrong before saying "I'm sorry" (a standard percentage), but now you'll admit fault at 27 percent. The other's PAP is irrelevant to you. *You* are apologizing for *your* part—even if you were provoked, even if you were defending yourself, even if you acted out of hurt, even if you were pushed to your limit.

Humbling? Without a doubt. Virtue building? Without a doubt. As your PAP drops, even the most inveterate apology resister may notice. Who knows, maybe his PAP will begin to drop, even if by fractions?

"I may say sorry, but I don't feel sorry." Well, before there were relationship gurus, philosophers instructed, "First form the habit; the desire will follow." Our "go with your feelings" culture has reversed that wisdom. Our emotions must point in the right direction before we act in that direction. We don't behave as we should because the companion feeling is absent.

One doesn't need the right feeling to act right. Even when a particular feeling only weakly accompanies some behavior, repetition of the behavior builds the feeling. Given enough repetition, the gap between "I do it" and "I feel it" will close.

No question, in the fury of an altercation, the dominant emotion may be anything but apologetic. Any sort of heartfelt, "I'm sorry I used that word" might feel out of reach.

On to Plan B: Apologize later, when the emotions have subsided. Do delayed damage control. At the peak of hard and hurt feelings, no way, no how can you force out those distasteful words, particularly if your PAP hovers under 10 percent (according to your clear-eyed assessment). "Better later than never" is good apology guidance, whether it's three minutes or three days.

What if "I'm sorry" is not a labor for you but is for someone close to you? Your apology ratio to hers is 5:1 in a good month. You may conclude: She's prideful; she's full of herself; she thinks he's special; she feels superior.

The opposite is true. Again, the fewer the apologies, the greater the feelings of self-doubt. Understanding this will lessen your frustration at another's apology aversion. It will also soften you. It is easier to forgive those who struggle within themselves than those who sound pride-driven or superior.

Forgive me for repeating myself, but an honest apology is not only addressed to another person. It is also addressed to God. You are telling Him, "However many and repeated my flaws, I trust fully in Your forgiveness."

17

Being a "So?" Christian

My sister is two years younger than I am, though she claims it's more like twelve years. Growing up we bickered, but no more than normal. About every seventeen minutes or so.

As the older and, in my mind, far more reasonable child, I tailored my arguments to the matter at hand. My sister had a pet comeback, one she delivered with flair, no matter the matter.

An illustration. Our mother makes a cake, saving an after-school piece for each of us. Getting home, I head straight for the refrigerator.

Me: Sue, where's my cake that Mom left in the refrigerator?

Sue: Isn't it in there?

Me: No, it's not in there, and is that icing on your cheek? Did you eat mine, too?

Sue: Maybe.

Me: Mom said three times last night that cake was for both of us.

Sue: So?

Me: I was looking forward to it all day.

Sue: So?

Me: You ate yours, and then you ate mine, too.

Thinking Like Jesus

Sue: So?

Me: That's not right. I'm telling Mom.

Sue: So?

I didn't realize it then, but in her go-to response, Sue gave me a technique for becoming a more easygoing Christian. By "easygoing," I mean "harder to rile up."

My rough estimate is that 73.167 percent (not that I keep track) of all my upset or hurt comes from something someone has said to or about me. That is, it comes by word. My immediate reaction is often similar to when my cake was gone: I want to set the person straight, to give her my side of things. "Why would you say that?" Or, "That doesn't make sense." Or, "Let me show you how you're wrong." If not aloud, in my thoughts.

Reasoning succeeds mostly with those who are ready to reason. Not only children but adults are moved regularly by something other than reason—impulse, emotion, self-interest. Consequently, 59.135 percent of the time, again my gross estimate, reason meets with denial or resistance.

A pessimistic perspective? It would seem to be a reasonable one, given our fallen nature. Sometimes someone's idea of reason is another's idea of unreasonableness. What then?

Take a lesson from my sister, with one significant adjustment. She voiced a saucy, "So?" But you can keep your "So?" in your head. "So?" may be a pet kid comeback; it's not a mature way to win over an adult.

Anybody can say anything about anybody at any time for any reason. Upon hearing something you don't like hearing, first ask: Is what I'm hearing possibly true? If so, scrutinize yourself. It's not time for indifference. It is time for self-honesty. On the other hand, if, after some soul-searching, you conclude that the other person's words are coming from insecurity, misperception, or just plain nastiness, then a silent "So?" may be your only and best answer.

Being a "So?" Christian

"So?" does not mean "I don't care what you think because I don't care about you." Rather, it means, "I'm not going to be offended or thrown off-kilter by words that are undeserved." "So?" is a small word with big benefits. It says, "I realize that people can be hurtful, but I don't have to let them hurt me."

My Christian obligation is to consider others' words as honestly as I can — and, if true, to let those words change me. If not true, to remain emotionally unmoved by them. And to repeat to myself "So?" as needed.

18

High Standards Equal Rebellion?

I attended a conference at which a therapist, whose area of interest was adolescence, intoned authoritatively, "We all know that teens will rebel if a parent's standards are too high." Heads nodded knowingly. I stared stone-faced—something I'm good at; I've raised teens. Had I been feeling a little more rebellious, I would have countered, "No, we all don't know that, and all teens don't rebel." Call it my inner adolescent.

How such a counterintuitive piece of nonsense has gained so much traction among both parents and professionals is bewildering. (Just because someone gets paid for giving advice doesn't mean the advice is always good.) Indeed, of all the confidence-killing, morally constricting notions that assault parents these days, this one gets my vote as ranking among the worst. How's that for psychological sugarcoating? Talk about putting a governor on parental standards. "It's okay to set your bar—just not too high."

When experts assert this, they aren't limiting themselves to academics, sports, music, competitive powerlifting. Certainly, in the arena of skills, a parent can push too hard, living through his child, melding his ego into the child's achievement. Push too hard here, ignoring the signs of pushback, and kids can rebel, even shut down.

"High standards risk rebellion" is routinely aimed, however, at the shaping of character: Don't over-elevate your moral expectations, or Faith may maneuver around or outright reject them, seeing them as unreasonable and unreachable.

Yes, if a parent is dictatorial and morally harsh, he does court major opposition. An unfeeling code of conduct can veer too close to "My way or the highway, kid." It has been said, wisely, that "rules without relationship can breed rebellion."

There is a critical distinction between strong parenting with lots of love and strong parenting with little love. Too often, the distinction is ignored. The warning is that no matter how loving a parent, expecting too much good behavior is asking for psychological trouble. The morals she's striving to instill will be the very things to fuel her child's immorality.

How does one relax standards that are too lofty? "Truman, I'd like you to be honest all the time, but that does seem a bit rigid. So, how about a goal of only two lies per week, three if they're small." "Rocky, I would hope that you wouldn't mistreat your sister, but I realize that's a false hope. How about if you limit yourself to calling her two names a day and tormenting her every other day?"

All-the-time honesty or part-time honesty? No bullying at all, or a little every so often to quench the urge? To compromise a standard, one has to allow exceptions to it, and it is the exceptions that weaken its spirit.

"High standards" is a relative phrase—relative to a group norm. A standard can look extreme as group standards slip. These days, what is moral is often poll-driven: If most are following a lower standard, they set the reigning standard. If the norm is unhealthy, though, what is healthy is actually out of the norm. That is: too high.

High Standards Equal Rebellion?

Once upon a time, parents instinctively understood that imparting and enforcing standards was a top priority. The higher the standards, the better. It was a *lack* of standards that led to poor living. In our newfound enlightenment, the reverse is now proclaimed. Standards too high above the group standard can lead to their rejection.

Do kids push against rules and expectations? They wouldn't be kids if they didn't. They neither fully understand nor appreciate them. Young minds judge some of the most reasonable moral principles as too unreasonable for their liking. They survey their peer landscape with its looser freedoms and challenge, "How can all those parents be wrong and you be right?" A good answer: "They are, and I am." Indeed, being parent-compared is one sign that a parent's standards are at a healthy level. Thank the kids for the vote of confidence.

Perhaps more than ever before, many young adults are forsaking, in part at least, their parents' moral teachings. One interpretation: The kids couldn't live up to them, so they renounced them. Mostly an erroneous conclusion. Grown children abandon the Faith and its morals for a myriad of reasons — godless cultural forces preeminent among them. Shedding the "heavy" yoke of binding standards is not high on the list. Though it may be cited as a reason, it routinely hides other reasons that have little to do with "I just couldn't measure up."

This myth finds a stereotypical face in the preacher's child, who, as everyone knows, is the sneakiest, most fly-under-the-moral-radar kid in the congregation. Nodding yes to dad's teaching, he lives a no. What most everyone knows, though, turns out to be more talk than reality. Most preachers' kids grow up reflecting, not rejecting their upbringing. According to one study, pastor's kids are no more likely to walk away from the faith than other Christian teens. False ideas are sustained by the exceptions that do fit the stereotype.

Thinking Like Jesus

This nutty notion can cripple your resolve to take stands that you know are right—but because of second-guessing, you wobble. After all, Dorothy already thinks she has the Wicked Witch of the East for a mother and Attila the Hun for a father. So you'll only push her in the opposite moral direction with your God-guided absolutes. Best to compromise here and there to make your standards appear more reachable.

A high standard is an ideal, a goal to strive for. Jesus said, "You … must be perfect, as your heavenly father is perfect" (Matt. 5:48). Perfect? Such a nonnegotiable word. Did Jesus not realize psychologically what He was saying? Was He teaching that the only path to heaven lies in keeping impossibly high precepts? Or was He encouraging us to stretch toward those precepts?

It is not godly standards that breed rebellion. It is one's style in teaching and enforcing those standards. Your children are not walking a raised moral plane by themselves. You're walking alongside them. Everyone is raised better when the standards are elevated.

19

Unoffendable

"Unforgettable," sang Nat King Cole in his signature song. Christians should sing a similar signature song, "Unoffendable."

A trait that personifies our society is "prickliness." Taking harrumphing offense is the automatic response of many. College students retreat to "safe spaces" to hide from hearing anything contrary to their sense of things. Politicians delicately mouth ever-evolving, linguistically correct terms so as not to miff potential voters. Adolescents stand cyber-ready to retaliate in (un)kind to anyone who makes an "insensitive" post. A code of the streets warns, "Don't stare or even look at someone lest he feel challenged."

Behind all this peevishness is an inflated sense of self: "I'm competent; I'm good; I'm awesome; I'm cool." And everyone better recognize it. If I even sniff that you don't, I will quickly assert what I believe to be my due.

An overblown sense of "me" develops young. From preschool on, children are counseled to see themselves as wonderful simply because they affirm it to be so. From the Christian viewpoint they are indeed wonderful, as they are children of God. Still, how much self-declared self-inflation is good for you? How much is too much, and what effect does it have on personal relationships?

Thinking Like Jesus

As I've said throughout this book, my worth is not determined by me. My worth rests on an infinite word spoken by the Creator of the universe. Of all people, Christians should be the least easily offended, since we have a sense of who we are that comes from God Himself. This should help to insulate us emotionally from others' judgments of our abilities, competence, status, or value. Were it possible this side of heaven to fully know our value in God's eyes, we would be completely immune to offense.

An offense is a type of insult, a put-down of my religion, my character, my parenthood—in essence, something central to my person. And the more central, the more I feel demeaned. Ignoring or laughing off comments about my pitiful artwork isn't hard for me because since kindergarten I've known that I can't color within the lines. Call me a woefully inarticulate writer (You wouldn't, would you?), and I'm all too ready to defend myself. "So you think this is easy. Let's see you try it!"

There is a "How dare you?" aspect to taking offense. "How dare she say that about my children?" "How could he actually think that?" "Why would she not give me any credit for that?" It's taken as a lack of respect, an inaccurate view of me.

Offense also comes faster when it comes from someone who matters. "She's my mother. She should realize I . . ." It comes faster when what I most value is devalued. "I try so hard to be loving, and they accuse me of being judgmental."

To be offended means to expect recognition, or honor, or attention, or praise. None of these, however, are *due* to a follower of Christ. Again, our worth comes from being His follower, not from approval polls.

Only one person deserved no insults or derision whatever. Only one person truly had no personality flaws. Yet He received far more derision than I ever will. Is the student better than his master? Am I more deserving of respect than Jesus?

20

Too Many Kids

Our society has wrapped its arms around a new sexual code: If it feels good (or even if not), do it. "Between consenting adults," pretty much anything is celebrated. Pretty much anything, that is, except having babies in marriage. Well, having babies is okay, just keep the numbers down. Having more than the approved 1.86 children ranks up there with two other modern cultural sins—smoking and spanking.

The new commandment: Don't judge another's behavior—unless she's a mother of more than two (and especially if she also smokes or spanks). The rule is: Shun talking politics or religion, but feel licensed to offer unsolicited opinions about her most personal life decisions.

Christians believe children are souls from God. And they cooperate in bringing those souls into existence, giving of themselves for the well-being of each soul. It is deeply ironic, then, that the modern mindset has redefined this self-giving to more than two children as *selfishness*. (Three is permissible if "You're trying for your boy [or girl], right?") The more kids, the more one is suspected of being moved by emotional or spiritual greed, even pride. A mom of several kids told me she heard more than once, "What are you trying to prove?"

Thinking Like Jesus

Parents of "too many kids" also get accused of abusing the earth, soaking up natural resources, and depleting the rainforest. What's worse, with all their child deductions and credits, they aren't even paying their fair share of taxes! Basically, they keep adding people to an already over-peopled world. (One response to this censure is "How are you so sure you're not one of the 'too many'?")

No society in human history has enjoyed our level of abundance. Yet a standard objection to three or more children is strictly material: "How can you adequately care for them?" Meaning what? Food? Shelter? Cars? Bathrooms? Stuffed animals? The intangibles — love, affection, attachment — are not limited reservoirs. As one mother put it, "Love doesn't divide; it multiplies."

In one of my own self-doubting moments, at around child number six, I asked my wife, "How can I give each one enough individual attention?" She straightened me out, "Ray, that's why they have brothers and sisters." An insight confirmed every time I was the last pick in family kickball games.

During our adoption screening for our fourth child, the social worker asked, "Do you have sufficient bedrooms?" I was just about to answer, "Well, they have walls, a ceiling, beds, but no TV," until Randi shot me a look that said, "Don't say it, Ray." We did have three bedrooms, which seemed quite enough to me. If need be, Randi and I could sleep on the futon. Well, I could.

When our oldest daughter, Hannah, entered college, the orientation program counseled incoming students on how to adjust to a roommate. At which Hannah exclaimed, "Only one?" She had entered dormitory heaven.

The comments to "over-kidded" parents are predictably similar, old, and tired (even though everyone thinks they're clever). "Don't you have a TV?" "Have you figured out how this happens yet?" "Are you done?"

There is risk in cornering veteran mothers. These are women shaped by the daily unending questions of small humans.

"Is this all your family?" Of course not, our oldest is at home with the triplets.

"Haven't you ever heard of birth control?" Yes, I have. Why do you ask?

"Is your husband thinking of getting fixed?" I didn't think he was broken.

"Don't you think you have too many children?" Which one should I give back?

"I'm glad it's you and not me." I think my kids are glad, too. (Ouch.)

With every child, a parent doesn't automatically become saintlier. Many honestly lament, "Before I had kids, I was a much nicer person. Now I get mad faster and nag too much and talk too loud."

Just because children are gifts from God doesn't mean they are always easy to live with. Consider the average juvenile. He enters the world immersed in himself. Others are here to meet his needs—right now. He wants what he wants when he wants it. His conscience slowly evolves over many years, at least one hopes so. He is ruled by impulses that with maturity and heavy parental effort come to be somewhat bridled. And then we call him "strong-willed" or "a challenge." Huh?

One saint, upon visiting her sister's large family, is reported to have confessed her need to get back to the convent, with grown-ups, where it was quieter and where there was less temptation to irritation. (Probably smelled better, too.) As one wag once put it, "Being a parent means being prepared to be awakened at 4:00 a.m. on Saturday morning with, "What's a word that rhymes with the letter *J*?"

If God says kids are a blessing, then they are. "Whoever receives one such child in my name receives me" (Matt. 18:5). Despite what society, relatives, and smaller families say. If you feel moved to respond to critical remarks, start with sweetness. "We love kids; we couldn't be more grateful; we want whatever God gives us."

Sometimes a good response is no response—a smile, a shrug, a blank look. Blank looks say, "I don't understand your point." Besides, who can expect an intelligent riposte from anyone who lives with that many children?

In the end, what most wins over the naysayers are the children themselves. Parents of plenty of kids typically invest plenty of time, effort, and moral wisdom in raising their families. They have asked for the "overload." In time, others will not observe children who have been psychologically shortchanged. Quite the contrary, they will observe young people who are maturing into individuals admired by those same people who once didn't understand their parents.

21

Are You Me?

A graduate-school exam asked me, "What qualities personify a good counselor?" Thinking back, the question probably avoided the word "good," which would have been called too "value laden" and thus judgmental. It most likely opted for a word like "effective." Nonetheless, at the risk of making value judgments, let's stick with "good."

Some researchers have posed three qualities that make for a good counselor: warmth, genuineness, and accurate empathy. Warmth is kind concern, the presence of caring. Genuineness is sincerity and honesty. To use a trendy term, it is being authentic. Who one appears to be is who one is. Accurate empathy is the ability to identify and vicariously experience the emotions and thoughts of another.

Empathy, both inside and outside therapy, is thought to elevate the value of advice. The feeling is that, for someone to give wise counsel, he should be able to relate personally to the problem and thus be emotionally sensitive to whomever he is advising.

Some years ago I was a guest on a television show about oppositional adolescents. I suggested having a teen write an essay on respect for each bout of disrespect. With a look of surly disrespect, a mother of teens challenged me, "Do you have any children?" "Yes," I replied, "I have six," which was our family size at the time. At that, the audience let out a shout that clearly meant: "Gotcha!"

Not to be upstaged, she countered with, "Are any of them teenagers?" "Not yet," I answered, whereupon the audience turned their "Gotcha" back on me, as she sat back with an expression that said, "Checkmate." Clearly, she believed that to give her, or anyone, good guidance, you need to have worn her shoes—or, in this case, raised teenagers, particularly, disrespectful ones.

As an intern at a VA hospital, I ran a group for men diagnosed with mental disorders. The very first session, I was accosted by a young man who had spent time in prison. "Have you ever been in jail?" "No." (Does grad school count?) "Then what can you tell me?" he demanded. I answered, "True, I've never been in prison. And that may be why I do have something to tell you. How and why I've managed to avoid getting in trouble with the law may have some value to you."

Not only have I never been incarcerated, but I am not a child of divorce; I was not a troubled adolescent; I have never been addicted to drugs; and, as far as I'm aware, I am not mentally ill. Neither am I an octogenarian, an atheist, or a woman. If my practice were confined to subjects with which I have direct, personal experience, I would be pretty much limited to seeing clients who are middle-aged white males, married for thirty-plus years to the same wife, with ten kids (the final number—I wonder if that would have made any difference to my fellow TV guest or the audience).

My first book, *You're a Better Parent Than You Think!*, was written not only before I had children, but before I was married. My childrearing ideas were based not only upon my education but also upon years of working with parents. For the most part, the book reflects how I think today. My post-children books contain ideas based on decades of experience, along with the welter of emotions and stories that I accumulated through fatherhood. Still, the bulk of my guidance comes from contacts with countless parents more than from my own family. (Besides, all ten of my children are adopted, so that would mean I have never "experienced" my own biological children.)

Can a priest give guidance about strengthening a marriage? About better child raising? About dating? About dying? *Has he ever died?* Taken to its logical extreme, very few people could offer high-quality advice to very, very few people. They simply don't have the necessary emotional "knowledge" about what the other person is going through.

How did this "You need to be me" notion gain so much social traction? People generally speak from their own lived circumstances, whether about in-laws, finances, kids, or marriage itself. Consequently, they want lived experience from another, with the mistaken belief that it lends more credibility and sensitivity.

Suppose I'm a counselor who has had three failed marriages. Someone comes to me because her marriage is failing. On one hand, she trusts me to "understand" her circumstances better, since I have "been there." On the other, my attitude may be seriously jaded by my own marital struggles and all its complications. My experience may enhance the accuracy of my counsel — or it may degrade it.

I assume the mother who challenged my essay strategy was facing major teen defiance; after all, she was on a TV show about oppositional kids. She also flat-out defied my suggestions. When someone reflexively reacts with, "You don't know what it's like," it means she really isn't interested in counsel. This retort, in my experience, is more likely to be used by those who would most benefit from good advice.

I've discovered a nearly foolproof way to guarantee that my advice will not be so discounted. All I need to do is figure out what someone wants me to say, and then say it. Very few people will reject sympathy, approval, or affirmation because someone has not navigated circumstances like theirs. In short, as long as what I'm saying makes someone feel better, I'll get a good hearing. If it doesn't, I might be short-circuited with a "Well, you've never ..."

Should you be tempted to use the "Are you me?" defense, consider several points. First, someone's experience may allow him to sympathize and offer comfort, but that is no guarantee that the advice will be helpful to you. Second, sound advice can come from anyone at any time, regardless of whether they've walked in your shoes. Third, sometimes someone can give great advice for the very reason that he has *avoided* your circumstances. And finally, advice must be judged by its merits, not necessarily by who's offering it. Parents know: Even a five-year-old can say helpful and insightful things. For sure, he hasn't experienced much of life yet.

22

I Don't Want To

Therapists know: Anything can be a justification to avoid something you really don't want to do. A justification is distinct from a reason. A reason can be a legitimate explanation: "I'm giving less to the Church because I had to take a lower-paying job." This is distinct from an excuse: "I'm giving less to the Church because I gave extra last year."

A justification is a faux reason. It has a ring of validity. "I'm giving less to my church because it spends too much money on remodeling." It hides the real motive: "I just want to give less."

Long before insight psychotherapy, philosophers counseled: Know yourself. Meaning, know why you act as you do. A noble pursuit. Sorting through one's motives, unfortunately, does not come easily or naturally. Routinely they are a knot of the obvious and the obscure. What's more, I have layers of defenses serving my ego. My instinct is not to look too unfavorably at my conduct and intent.

"Father talks too much about money." "The church doesn't need a new organ." "The collection is up, anyway." "I give to other charities, too." Any of these can be justifications for the actual reason: I don't want to give more than my fair share.

Thinking Like Jesus

Justification can foster circular reasoning. "I'm not going to apologize." Why not? "He won't accept it." How do you know? "He hasn't in the past." He might this time. "He might, but I'm still not going to apologize." Why not? "He won't accept it."

When parents ask me for discipline help, knowing how to direct them is often the easier step. The harder step is persuading them to act. "We've tried that, and it doesn't work." "He'll just get worse." "He won't listen." "That's too strict." "If I'm consistent, I'll be disciplining constantly." "That's not my style."

Early psychotherapists put a name on this phenomenon: resistance. It is the defense against insight or guidance. It's the emotional pushback. But why would someone seeking guidance resist the very thing he seeks? Because he doesn't actually want it.

Oh, he may want some sort of help. It depends on what kind or how much. What will it ask of him? How high is the cost in energy or will? He wants change, but not if that means changing himself.

If I am the god of my life, "I don't want to" is a guiding principle, perhaps the premier one. My goal is to maximize my pleasure and minimize my pain. Why would I do something I don't desire to do, or don't feel like doing, or have to force myself to do? If I don't want to spend any time around my obnoxious brother-in-law, I won't. If I don't want to compliment my wife, who doesn't compliment me, I won't. To quote three-year-olds, "If I don't want to, I don't have to."

If Jesus is the God of my life, "I don't want to" needs to be squashed. I may not be inclined to give to charity ("I give enough"), to visit elderly Aunt Martha ("A few minutes after I leave, she forgets I was even there"), to take a Bible study course ("It's right in the middle of Monday Night Football"), to listen longer to boring Uncle Fred ("That will just encourage him"), or to discipline more calmly ("They listen only if I get mad"). Nonetheless, if God wants me to, His will supersedes mine. For any one charitable act, I can concoct several reasons to resist it. Call them resistance rationales.

On any given day, exercise is not high on my "to do" list. Yet, I know it has benefits I want. These outweigh (no pun intended) any "I don't feel like it today." Likewise, acting for Christ may not be my first impulse, but it will bring benefits I can't always anticipate. Doing what is right and good, ignoring any resistance rationales, can morph an "I really don't want to" into an, "I'm glad I did."

"I don't feel like it" equals "I don't want to." In our feelings-saturated society, emotions rule. They reveal our "genuine" motives; thus, they shouldn't be questioned. If my feelings don't parallel what I should do (I won't *say* "sorry" until I *feel* sorry), my action is thought to be insincere and thereby meaningless. "I don't feel like it" lends emotionally credibility to "I don't want to."

"Follow your heart." Cliché guidance. The plot line to any number of maudlin, made-for-TV movies. The heart isn't always a good leader, though. "Follow your heart" implies that somewhere deep inside, beyond words and reason, lies the sure guide to the best end. Many failed marriages once followed the heart and ignored the head. The heart may declare either, "I want to" or "I don't want to," but both need to yield to "*I should.*"

"I'm not comfortable with that." A psycho-trendy phrase. It speaks to acting within one's "comfort zone." On one hand, a mature conscience forms a healthy comfort zone. One should feel unsettled at the thought of disobeying God's precepts. It's not okay to play solitaire on the computer during work time. No comfort zone should exist for surfing pornography.

On the other hand, comfort is not a good guide to good conduct. Visiting a nursing home, a funeral, a prison—any one of these can push someone out of her comfort zone. Following the Master asks us to do what discomfort, even anxiety, pushes us to avoid. He asks us to carry our cross. That can't possibly be always comfortable.

Thinking Like Jesus

"I don't want to" is ingrained in our self-oriented nature. That doesn't mean our better nature can't overcome it. We just have to want to.

Here are some ideas.

1. Know that what you think are your reasons may not be your reasons. Look for other motives that could be ruling and are being covered up by flimsy rationales.

2. Do some self-counseling. If all your justifications could be answered (Aunt Martha does remember you were there, and she lives for visitors), would you still not visit? If every objection could be legitimately countered, would you fall back on "I still don't want to"?

3. If "I don't want to" is talking, answer it with, "So what?" That is: Whether or not I *want to* is irrelevant. The question is, "Would Christ want me to?"

Doing what you don't want to do, because it's good and right, will lead you to what you really want to do: become a better disciple of Christ.

23

Mad at Whom?

Preschoolers sing a song that begins, "If you're happy and you know it, clap your hands.... If you're happy and you know it, then your face will surely show it ..."

Psychologists could sing, "If you're angry and you know it, let them know.... If you're angry and you know it, then your words will surely show it ..." To keep relationships transparent, so the lyrics say, emotions are best expressed, be they happy or mad.

It's a law of physics: To reduce the pressure in a vessel, give it an outlet. As with an old-fashioned tea kettle, when the water reaches a boil, it seeks release. That's its nature.

Long ago Sigmund Freud said something similar about the nature of the mind: Anger and its companion, aggression, can build up to a boiling point. They need to be vented, lest they wreak havoc on their vessel, the human psyche. He called this venting *catharsis*.

Over time the notion of catharsis gained a lot of steam and diffused into the popular psyche. It seemed so sensible, so basic, so, well, scientific. And there is some truth to it: Stuffing down resentments and anger over time *can do* physical damage. Harboring raw feelings inside can ultimately lead to a breakdown somewhere in the body. Talking the anger through can be healthy for both the psyche and the body—given a major qualifier.

Whatever anger is pushing for release, the release itself needs to be free from anger. Let someone know how you feel, but don't be nasty about it. Use cautious judgment about when, where, with whom, and how often to "share."

Anger gets hotter when we nurture three thoughts: that another has been unfair to us; that he has made our lives unduly difficult; or that he could have helped us but didn't. Put simply: People are not acting as we would like them to.

Christians recognize that God is more than a little involved in life. So, it's not uncommon for Him to become the object of our anger. After all, He is the Creator and Designer of all existence. If He wanted, He could alter things for (what we think would be) the better for any of us.

I started college studying engineering. All the mathematical equations have pretty much faded from my mind. One axiom has stuck with me, though: To correctly solve any formula, one has to have as many equations as variables. Anything less can lead to a wrong answer.

God alone knows every single variable involved in every single life circumstance. He has complete knowledge of complexities we couldn't even imagine. Compared with His understanding of life, we are barely first-year engineering students. No, that's not quite accurate: We aren't even infants.

To be angry at God is to say, "God is not acting as I would like." Either, "I see all this as clearly as God does, and I don't agree with Him," or "I may not understand everything, but what I do understand, I don't like."

Some anger at being hurt by life is understandable. The emotion is misdirected, however, when God becomes the target. This impulse arises from a faulty view of God's nature.

Mad at Whom?

God isn't like some ancient mythological deity who slings lightning bolts at people who irritate him. Neither does He play cosmic chess with humans as pawns. God *can't* create evil or wrong, as it would be completely contrary to His very being. Therefore, to be angry with God is to blame Him for something He didn't do. It gets the main variable in the equation wrong.

"God may not be causing my trouble, but He could stop it. Why doesn't He? Where is He?"

My son Andrew was born with a cleft lip and palate, which required several operations to correct. Around age two, he needed to have blood drawn for an upcoming surgery. Because he was so young, his veins were hard to find. Repeated needle sticks were attempted, as Andrew screamed and struggled against the restraining nurses. He didn't know who his captors were, and his fear magnified his pain.

"Please let me hold him for you," I offered. As the nurse continued to probe, Andrew looked up at me with teary eyes that conveyed, "Daddy, why are you allowing these people to hurt me?" All I could think was, "Andrew, if you only knew what I know."

How often must God think, "If you only knew what I know." Getting angry at God for what I don't know, can't foresee, and can barely understand is, in essence, acting as a spiritual preschooler. I believe that what little I can see for the moment is all there is or will be to see. I believe my picture is as complete as God's.

Anger at God may stem from the "buddy" factor—that is, that God is my best friend and that I feel very comfortable with Him. So, as I would toward a close friend, I feel I can and should express my feelings. True, God is our best friend. But that isn't the full measure of our relationship. He is the Master of the universe, Who knows all and can see infinity. Therefore, to react toward Him as one would to another human being would be to mischaracterize the relationship dramatically. It places us on a relatively equal footing. Yes, a friend; yet, far, far more.

Thinking Like Jesus

Anger at God may reveal a sense of spiritual entitlement. "I've been faithful. I try to act as God wants me to. And then He lets this happen to me." Or: "I'm playing by God's rules, and this is my reward?"

Living for God is its own reward, now and forever. I'm in no position to set the terms for how exactly my life should unfold. Earthly existence is not merely a kind of prologue to heavenly existence.

My anger at God is most intense when I am the one personally to suffer misfortune. I can be aware of widespread human tragedies, and I might question God, but I do not get incensed toward Him. Let tragedy directly affect me, or someone I love, and then the questions morph into anger. It's one thing to see suffering; it's quite another to experience it. Now it's personal.

When I can't identify a person who seems to be responsible for my pain, or when life itself seems to have conspired against me, it is tempting to see God as the conductor of my misery. Right thinking must then talk sense to my misdirected emotions. God isn't to blame, nor is He there to cure every evil. Was Jesus angry at His Father for the Cross? No: He understood it was all for a far greater purpose.

God's infinite perspective and goodness is ever ready to bring healing from hurt, good from bad, growth from pain. Our cooperation helps Him to do so. And cooperation begins by not getting mad at God.

24

Ninety Percent Obedient

Suppose you are the parent of a teen who approaches you with this bargain: "Mom [Dad], I've come to realize that your ways are good ways for me to live. So I intend to follow them—as long as I agree with them, which is most of the time, I'd say, about 90 percent. When I don't agree, I'll ignore them and do what I want. You should be pleased because I obey a lot more than most kids my age!"

Would you think this child as obedient as he thinks he is? When I present this scenario to parents, few agree with the teen. As long as he can decide when and how to cooperate, his authority ranks above his parents' authority, no matter how often he actually does cooperate. Put simply, *he chooses*.

We can draw a parallel to Christ's Church and Her followers. We are called to obey Her, as our mother, for our own short- and long-term well-being. And, for the most part, we do: We receive the sacraments, pray, attend Mass, support charities, obey the law, live by the Golden Rule—all with some consistency. What if we *don't* agree with Her? Do we still obey? If not, what is our percentage of disobedience? For many Catholics, it is highest in the spheres of marriage and sexuality: divorce, contraception, abortion, fornication, masturbation, homosexuality.

Thinking Like Jesus

The thinking goes like this: If I don't see the reasons for a teaching and I don't concur with it, then I don't have to abide by it. I will abide when doing so is agreeable to me, but that's the extent of it.

Ironically, while I call the teen's 90 percent rate disobedient, I call my 90 percent obedient. After all, on the balance I obey lots more than I disobey, and I have a generally obedient disposition. That's what matters, isn't it? Ninety percent is an A grade, or at least a high B, in most courses.

Now, one might argue that the parallel breaks down because a parent has full authority as long as a minor child lives in her home, while the Church's "children" are mainly adults who are free to decide how to act. True, they are. The Church forces no one to obey. But if She is founded by Christ, as Catholics believe, then She has far *more* authority than a parent. Her authority extends over Her children's lives, from birth to death, and not just prior to age eighteen.

When I walked away from the Catholic Church, it wasn't because I was upset at Her teachings or Her people. No, my motive was simple, if wrongheaded: God is and will remain God; Jesus is and will remain Jesus; now I'm moving onto a congregation that better suits my spiritual tastes. I was the teen in the above example. At my most distant from Her, I still thought like the Church 90 percent of the time. But when I didn't, I ignored her or disobeyed, arrogating *to myself* the authority of how best to follow Christ.

Just like the teen who decides when to obey his parents has, in truth, replaced them with himself, so do the believers who choose when to obey God replace Him with themselves.

The thinking of the old breed of atheist makes logical sense, even if the premise is wrong: There is no God, so I can do what I want—up to a legal limit anyway. Or, to use the words of Fyodor Dostoyevsky's character, Ivan Karamazov, "If there is no God, everything is permissible."

The new breed of atheist, on the other hand, says, "There is a God, and He thinks just like me." The ranks of the new kind of atheist dwarf those of the old atheists. They believe in God, often the God of Christianity—but they decide when to agree with Him.

If the Catholic Church is my mother, then, like a loving mother, She knows what is good for me and what will hurt me. I am not Her obedient child when I follow Her only when I agree with Her; I am her obedient child when I follow even when I disagree, trusting in Her wisdom over mine.

As an adolescent, I sometimes didn't understand my parents' thinking or methods. I understand now. The Church is spiritually raising me, and the last thing I want is to remain Her unruly adolescent.

25

Spiritual Correctness

A confidence-corroding notion permeates parenting these days. It is being fueled by a proliferation of experts and their theories. Call it "psychological correctness." It says that there are psychologically correct ways to communicate, discipline, supervise — in short, to raise a child. Use savvy reasoning, and Dusty will brush his teeth before mold sets in. Communicate via active listening "I-messages," and Oxford will complete his English paper before summer break. Design a cutting-edge sticker-reward chart, and Eve will accept bedtime without a bad time.

Follow expert guidance, the idea goes, and you will be well on your way to an emotionally satisfying, Hallmark-card family life. As the magazine headlines declare, we've uncovered the "secrets" to super childrearing. Which raises the question: Did all those generations prior to ours have to stumble along psychologically, oblivious to all these "secrets"?

The experts (me included) swarm talk shows and pour out countless articles and books every year. We are the gurus of parenting, at least for those willing to heed us. While our advice can be helpful, its net effect — confusion — however unintended, has nonetheless been real. It has generated second-guessing, needless worries, and an erosion of authority.

The basics of good parenting—love, common sense, firm discipline, moral judgment—all too often yield to a search for the knowledge of "proper" techniques and psychological prescriptions.

Even if "new and improved" strategies could ensure successful childrearing, one reality won't change: *The experts can't agree on what the right strategies are.* In almost every realm of childrearing—discipline, supervision, communication, academics, relationships with peers—the advice differs and is regularly contradictory.

Most faith-guided parents recognize that most secular experts don't think as they do, nor do they adhere to the same moral worldview. A few examples: Self-esteem tops humility; spanking is evil; high standards breed rebellion; homeschooling stunts socialization; large families shortchange children.

While a parent may recognize the traps of psychological correctness, she still may be misled by another version of it. Call it "spiritual correctness"—the belief that there are ways, if not to guarantee, at least to make it very likely, that a child raised in the Faith will remain in the Faith. Receive the sacraments; attend church faithfully; pray often; associate with like-minded families; educate in a Catholic or homeschool; live the example. The result of faith-filled living should be a child who seeks God into adulthood.

Don't misread me. This is not at all to argue that the odds of faithful parents raising a faithful child are slightly better than a coin flip. The odds are certainly dramatically higher. It is rather to argue against the notion that if the outcome is less than what was hoped for, then somehow the parenting was spiritually deficient.

Parents who watch their children leave their family's beliefs regularly blame themselves, scouring the past for hidden flaws. What could I have done better? More praying? More books about lives of the saints? Better answers to moral questions? Praying the

Rosary in Aramaic instead of in English, kneeling instead of sitting on the couch?

Do you live on a farm or small town in 1880? If so, the odds are high that your grown children will embrace your religion. For much of Christian history, except during periods of persecution, children generally stayed with what they were raised with. The family, clan, or tribe was the unchallenged teacher.

Do you live in the United States in the twenty-first century? Have you raised your family here in the past thirty years or so? Then surveys tell the story: Young adults are moving away from their parents' religion in unprecedented numbers.

The soul-misshaping forces of our irreligious society are everywhere and relentless: television, social media, movies, music, celebrities, academia, advertising. The message "God doesn't have a voice here" actively and seductively works against the voice of parents. Even when homes work to lock the ugliness out, like a vapor it seeps in to influence how a young person thinks, feels, and believes. It seeks to shape him in its image.

Despite all that, parents hold a powerful hand. Parents remain the main guides. What moves one child closer to God and another further away, though, is still somewhat of a mystery. Grace, free will, personality, circumstances—all interplay with a parent's guidance to direct a child's faith journey.

"Spiritual correctness" is all the more ensnaring when a parent witnesses others who have raised God-seeking offspring. The natural inclination is to attribute this to their home life and religious practices. What exactly did they do that I didn't? Maybe little. Again, personality and life factors may have cooperated with these parents. A call to the priesthood or religious life is God's. He has the perfect formulas, not we.

Most God-loving parents are not spiritually flawed. Some do deeply regret embracing the Church later in their parenting. If only they had started toward God sooner, they wonder. Still, to know God later is infinitely better than never to know Him. And the children now live with a better parent, one who prays for them.

Suppose that Jesus were beside you, whispering perfect instructions into your ears every day. That would guarantee a faith-filled young person, wouldn't it?

To answer that, here is a series of simple "yes-or-no" questions that I present to parent groups:

Is there a God? Yes.

Is Christ God? Yes.

Was He sinless? Yes.

Could He perform miracles? Yes.

Did He have a perfect understanding of human nature? Yes.

Slowly and deliberately I ask, "Could He get most people to follow Him?"

A pensive silence drifts through the group, as nearly all answer, "No."

One more question: If the God-man Himself couldn't get most people to follow Him, why do we think we can do better? I don't know about you, but I can't do miracles. I can't even do a cheap card trick.

Spiritual correctness collides with a core Christian belief: free will. Our Lord didn't impose His teaching on anyone. What makes us believe we can live and teach so convincingly that a young person will have no choice but to absorb it? Put another way, why do I think that if I'm a saint, I will raise a saint?

While you have no guarantee that all your devoted years will add up to a devoted young adult, you do have some assurance. First, the more faith-filled and loving you are, the more likely your kids will be drawn to your image. And second, leaving the Faith for a while doesn't mean leaving it always. Some children do return, more faithful than ever. Their parents' prayers nudged them toward the truth in which they were raised.

26

Proud of My Humility

Humility — the one virtue that, if you think you have it, you don't. Tongue planted firmly in cheek, I talk on my radio program about my years-long pursuit of the coveted humility award, which I finally captured this past year. My winning strategy was simple: While the other contestants attended the finals, awaiting the judges' ruling, I stayed home, knowing that, were I to win the award and then accept it, I would automatically lose it. Tricky stuff, this humility.

What is humility *not*? It is not thinking of oneself as a spiritual worm, unworthy of God's or anyone else's love. It is not disavowing one's gifts and talents given by God. It's not swatting away compliments with an attitude that says, "I'm undeserving." In short, humility is not thinking less of oneself; it is thinking of oneself less.

The modern self-esteem movement has relentlessly devalued humility. What now matters most to one's psychological well-being is not a humble self-image, but a robust one. We all deserve stickers, trophies, and awards. Why? Because we do. I am a special person because I declare me so. It's critical to my emotional fitness to be always in tune with my own significance.

Christians agree — sort of. We are indeed good, valuable, and special, though not because we say so, but because God says so. He awards the life stickers that matter in the end. His declaration of our worth is true self-esteem. It never rises or falls with our social approval numbers or our accumulation of skills, achievements, and education. One can have a truly humble spirit while at the same time being fully self-assured of one's infinite value. Tricky stuff, this humility.

Humility parallels reality. It is a clear-eyed assessment not only of one's weaknesses and sins and failures, but also of one's strengths and virtues and successes. If I am a master chess player, then I am a master chess player. It's not a humble move to deny that. Should I lose to another player, it is right to admit, "He beat me. He may be the superior player." "He is better than I am" is honest. Humility parallels reality.

A humble spirit is not something that can be grasped in itself. It's the fruit of a mindset: gratitude for all God has dispensed, in talents, achievements, successes, maturity, morality. To humbly acknowledge any gift is to be ever mindful of the giver. Even the desire and effort to maximize those gifts derives from God's prompting.

Humility is not a virtue one can proclaim. "I feel so unworthy." "I'm not the sweet person you think I am." "If you knew me better, you wouldn't think I'm such a good Christian." Any of which may be a well-meant confession, but would a simple "Thank you" be humbler? It doesn't say, "Come to think of it, I am most deserving of this honor." It is a straightforward, "I appreciate your kindness."

Humility underlies all manner of admirable qualities. It leads to an easiness in sincerely uplifting others. Any impulse to compete, to measure up, to show myself superior, or to advertise my intelligence, knowledge, or competence is weaker. As you tell me about your vacation to Europe, I don't anxiously await my turn to regale you about my three vacations to Italy, with its two Swiss Guard-guided visits to the Vatican and my personal papal audience.

Proud of My Humility

Thinking of oneself less leads to thinking of others more. Have you ever met someone, chatted awhile, and formed a favorable first impression? Later you realized why: She was genuinely interested in you. Not nosey, but eager to hear all about your family, your job, your interests. She wanted to know the bits and pieces of who you are and was much less invested in giving you her story and opinions. Somehow she deftly kept the focus on you.

Such individuals are appealing, even if they unwittingly corrupt your humility by animating you to talk about yourself. They are anything but self-absorbed; they are other-absorbed. Humility is at the heart of likability.

Humility is a safeguard against insecurity, the sense of not being as good as another. It restrains my measuring myself against you, in faith, parenting, housekeeping, finances, lawn care, doubles badminton. Rather than looking at how I compare with others, humility nudges me to look at how I compare with what God wants of me. Of course, I'd better not think, "I must be pretty humble because I really don't compete with others all that much." Again, if you think you've got it, you don't.

A wistful ditty: "I want to be famous, so I can be humble about being famous. What good is my humility when I'm stuck in this obscurity?" The greater one's status in the eyes of the world, the greater the need to keep focused on the Author of it all.

Humility is a hedge against easy offendedness. It asks, "Who am I to expect respect or recognition for what I do?" Of course, it's human to want positives, but reality intrudes: We will never get them from everyone, consistently, always.

Humility doesn't demand. It tempers the expectation to be treated as well as I treat others—or as well as I think I treat others. It makes me less sensitive to critical remarks and hurtful conduct. It is the unspoken belief, "Who I am in God's eyes matters infinitely more than who I am in others' eyes."

Thinking Like Jesus

A willingness to forgive accompanies a humble spirit. Realizing my humanness, with all my faults, failures, and fumbles should lead to more tolerance of others' humanness. If I am merciful to me, I must be merciful to them. I am slower to judge when I know I too may be capable of similar conduct. Should I think, "I'm glad I'm not like that," then I've just lost a bit of humility and might have to exchange my award for a participation trophy.

One more time: Humility is seeing who one is through the eyes of all-seeing love—God. It does not seek to lift the self, contrary to modern psychological enlightenment. It seeks to "count others better than [oneself]" (Phil. 2:3). Do so, and you may be nominated for the Humility Award. Of course, you can't accept it. Tricky stuff, this humility.

27

The System Works

I once asked a priest, "What for you is the strongest evidence for the truth of the Catholic Faith?" Without hesitation he answered, "The system works."

What system? The Church hierarchy of authority? The sacraments? The worship practices? He meant the moral system—what the Church teaches as the best way to live. It's a system routinely at odds with the world's system.

People seek my counsel in various states of distress. While well aware that things have gone wrong, they are less aware of why. They might believe in Christian morals yet not understand how drifting from those morals has led to some of their life turbulence.

Early psychology was not so friendly to religion. Some theories went so far as to argue that Christian thinking made one neurotic—guilt-ridden, unhappy, emotionally stunted. As it comes to better understand the human condition, though, psychology is giving the old morals some respect.

My book *Back to the Family* summarized the findings of a nationwide search for strong families. State teachers of the year from all fifty states identified some hundred families as exceptional models of family life. In interviews parents and children were asked, in essence, "What is happening here? How are you doing this?" Religion came through prominently. "Core to these families' success was belief in a creator and living by his guidelines." For the most part, the teachers didn't know the families' religious views ahead of time. All they knew was what they saw: well-adjusted children.

Modern psychology is confirming what Christ and His Church have taught for millennia.

* * *

The Church teaches that divorce is contrary to God's law. It hurts young and old — if not immediately, then in time. And social-science research now teaches that divorce is bad for children; neither is it harmless for most adults.

A spouse may be convinced that leaving his marriage will prove to be a renewed path to happiness. Only later does he find that he exchanged known struggles for unknown ones.[1]

* * *

Jesus says, "Turn the other cheek." Don't return ill treatment for ill treatment. Let offense pass. Psychology says: The best response to offense may be no response. Let offense pass. Clinging to it only adds to one's agitation.

Some decades back a movement known as "assertiveness training" gathered steam. It asserted that one needs to decisively assert one's personal rights, more so when they are felt to be ignored or trampled. Granted, there are times when it's smart to stand up for oneself. Too much confronting of others' perceived or real insensitive conduct, however, can lead to social isolation. Rather

---

[1] See Linda Waite and Maggie Gallagher, "The Case for Marriage: Why Married People are Happier, Healthier and Better Off Financially" (New York: Broadway, 2001), 148.

than help, it hurts relationships. One can assert oneself into social obnoxiousness.

Excessive vigilance for my "rights" can also become a *self*-agitating habit. Rehearsed offense in my mind leads to rehearsed upset. Again, knowing when to ignore disrespectful words or conduct can be morally healthy, psychologically speaking.

* * *

A survey among elderly people asked about "positive life satisfaction." One finding related to life satisfaction was a "broad social network." One conclusion: the larger their network, the more support received. A second conclusion: A wider social network allows the elderly to serve others through volunteering, child care, mentoring, and other charity. Instead of receiving care, the elderly gave it. "It is more blessed to give than to receive": So said Jesus through St. Paul's recollection (Acts 20:35).

* * *

Gratitude is a highly commendable Christian virtue. Thankfulness has long been recognized as a good doctor for the soul. Recent research is concluding it's a good doctor for the body, too.

"If [thankfulness] were a drug, it would be the world's best selling product with a health maintenance indication for every major organ system."[2] Gratitude has been linked to better physical health, reduced blood pressure, improved pain threshold, as well as lower

---

[2] Dr. P. Murali Doraiswamy, researcher in brain and mind health, as quoted in articles at Mercola.com. See, for instance, "The Many Benefits of Expressing and Receiving Gratitude," Mercola, November 26, 2015, https://articles.mercola.com/sites/articles/archive/2015/11/26/expressing-gratitude.aspx.

overall stress and anxiety. Other research says that gratitude is the single best predictor of good relationships.[3]

* * *

Our society has embraced a sexual free-for-all. Long-standing Judeo-Christian standards for a proper sexual life are loosening to the point of unraveling. Is this "freedom" progressive, as its advocates claim, or regressive?

In two generations the out-of-wedlock birth rate has exploded from under 10 percent to over 40 percent, leaving more children without present fathers. Venereal diseases, multiplying in kinds and frequency, are more virulent and often incurable. Marital infidelity is a major cause for consistently high divorce rates. Among those under thirty-five, more couples are living together than are married. Children are far more likely to be abused, physically and sexually, by cohabiting boyfriends than by husbands. Those who live together before marriage have higher divorce rates, should they eventually marry.

A university survey of the sexual practices of several lifestyles found that not singles but committed married couples had the highest satisfaction. Sex is best expressed in marriage? Who would have guessed?

* * *

When God says, "Do it my way, it's better for you," He knows what He's talking about. He designed us and knows exactly what will lead to good living, not only spiritually but psychologically. In more and more places, psychological understanding and Christian understanding are converging. Rather than a skeptical view of Christian morality, psychology is assuming a more agreeable one. The system works.

---

[3] Dr. Joseph Mercola articles at Mercola.com.

28

Heated Exit

Any therapist worth his or her therapeutic salt has watched a client walk out in the middle of a session. Whether the client didn't like what the therapist said, or what she thought he said, or how he said it, or what she thought he meant — it happens. Sometimes the exit is frosty and wordless. Sometimes it's stormy, raining words that sour the air.

Such exits are not a complete surprise. Therapy routinely probes the intricacies of motives and conduct. There's always a chance that a psychological nerve can get pinched. Not everything clients hear will necessarily be affirming. However, some are there seeking professional confirmation: Tell me I'm right. Should that not happen, they question the worth of counseling.

I must be worth some salt, as I have had folks heatedly exit my office. Fortunately, the numbers are low, else I would need a mirror held up to my own persona.

Who has most recently departed my office, never to return? A parent pressed to reform his discipline? No. An anxious individual? No. A teen with temper troubles? A likely candidate, but again, no. Someone "forced" to counseling by a court? He might be tempted, but consequences constrain him. A spouse in marriage counseling?

Closer. A spouse who is Christian when the other is not so much, if at all. Bingo.

Here's a walkout replay. Wife presents herself as a committed Christian. She is active at church, has a circle of like-minded friends, and speaks of high moral standards. Her husband is lukewarm at best toward religion.

Do you expect more from your marriage than your husband does? "Yes." Do you wish he'd give more to the marriage? "That would be nice." Does he think he gives to the marriage? "Yes, but I don't think he does." Why? "Because he doesn't see marriage as I do, as a Christian one."

So far, so safe. The tension is about to follow. At some point, I make an unexpected observation: mature faith asks more of someone — more understanding, tolerance, forgiveness. Christian principles are lofty, guiding her even when her husband is not so guided. At this point, she thinks I am absolving her husband of his fair share of marital effort. She hears me saying she could do better, while not shining a light on his many faults. He is the one, she believes, who could do lots better. He is the more selfish, the one who needs to change more. Counseling is supposed to address *that*.

And counseling will address that. While both spouses want a stronger marriage, their ideas of what that means aren't meshing. Should I nudge both toward self-examination, the wife feels misunderstood and "blamed." Her Christian self-view is shaken. A core nerve is being pinched, so she ends the session abruptly.

Husbands walk out, too. But in faith-split marriages, more often than not, the wife is the more spiritual.

Aren't good marriages fifty-fifty? Both spouses giving equally to each other? Not always. Depending on the issue, the ratio can be 90:10, 60:40, or even 100:0. The proportions overall may balance out, but not uncommonly one spouse is more emotionally, and perhaps spiritually, invested than the other. To expect someone with little or no faith to live as though he does is asking for frustration and recurring disappointment.

If one spouse strives to be more selfless, couldn't the other settle further into selfishness? An old joke gives an answer. An elderly farmer is sitting in a church service when a vile, sulfur-smelling creature explodes onto the scene. People panic and race toward the doors — all except the farmer, who sits unperturbed.

The creature does his best to terrorize, hissing, "Do you know who I am?"

"Yep."

"Aren't you afraid of me?"

"Nope."

"Why not?"

"Been living with your sister for forty years."

The point? Unless one is living with Satan or his spouse, living better *for Christ* is the best way to move a spouse to live better *for you*, even if inch by lurching inch.

There is a long-standing rule of marriage that I made up for this book. It's the Law of Reciprocity: Treat your spouse well, and she will treat you well. If you respect her, she will respect you. If you give affection, you will get affection. If you listen more, you will be heard more. This law is not perfect, though. It works best when both spouses are operating from the same value system. When not the case, a double standard can intrude, with one spouse feeling cheated. Her good efforts are not getting a good return, which can then fuel resentment, even ill will.

Christians live by a higher law: the law of charity. Relying on God's ever-present support, I am obliged to act better toward another than he acts toward me. I might very much hope that a loved one will do unto me as I do unto her, but that is not my due. My conduct in any relationship is moved by God's ways, independent of another's ways. Unless similar Christian impulses guide my spouse, much of my reward may have to come from a higher relationship.

Poll one hundred people, "Who is the better spouse in my marriage?", and you may get seventy-four votes. The better polling question is, "Am I living up to the standards I profess?" Should the approval numbers drop, ponder why. It's not a time to turn and walk out.

29

More Faith, Better Mood?

Religion and psychology intersect at depression: If I had more faith, would I be less depressed? Or, if I had more faith, would I be in a better mood?

That depends. (Precision is my forte.) Depression wears many faces. Its causes are varied and complex, intertwined with one's personality. Some depression, a minority, is biochemical. It is grounded in faulty brain chemistry. Medical science is just beginning to unravel where and how. Strong faith may have only a weak effect here. The mind is just not working right. And an omniscient God takes all that into account.

Some depression follows a life crisis—a loved one's passing, a fractured marriage, an illness, financial ruin. Faith may lessen the grip of the crisis, but may not lead all the way to, "I'm fine now, because I know God will work everything out for me." Strong faith or not, the impact of adverse life events can take a toll.

So, "more faith equals less depression" is not an absolute formula. Emotional heaviness may take time to decrease even as faith increases. Expecting otherwise can lead to spiritual self-doubt or, worse, a shaken faith. "I've played by God's rules, and still He lets this happen to me."

Thinking Like Jesus

Most depression is born and raised by how we think. Our thoughts are the parents of our emotions—how we interpret circumstances, how we read others, how we judge ourselves. Why is it that nearly identical hardships can rob one person of all joy while only temporarily troubling another? Much depends on how each interprets and understands the meaning of those hardships.

The power of thoughts to raise or lower emotions can be immediate and dramatic. Picture yourself jammed inside a crowded bus shelter. People are crunched into one another's spaces. Wind is gusting cold rain into the shelter. The bus is late, and your mood is getting drenched. While being jostled, what feels like the point of an umbrella starts to jab your heel. The pain is magnified by a cascade of thoughts. "What's with this joker? Is this his idea of fun? Does he only care about his own comfort? What about the rest of us?" Each jab brings more jolting thoughts.

You've had enough. Lurching around to give the weapon wielder a cease-and-desist glare, you see an elderly blind woman using her cane to stay oriented in the shifting mass of bodies. What happens to your building irritation? Instantly it vanishes. Other emotions follow from reality—sheepishness, perhaps guilt.

We are always interpreting the meaning of what happens to us and within us. Erroneous interpretations can turn one's mood darker. The thoughts themselves may not be sinful. Still, they can color one's demeanor, sometimes all the way to depression.

It is not weak faith that usually underlies depression. "Is there a God? Where is He in my life? Does He even care?" It is more often weak patterns of thinking. Uncovering and correcting misthinking can actually strengthen one's faith. The relationship is straightforward: Better thinking leads to better faith.

Professional counseling is one avenue toward better thinking. Another is self-counseling. Think about your own thoughts. Analyze them. Challenge them. What is coursing through my mind right now? Could I be misunderstanding this person? Is there a more accurate way to look at this event, this circumstance? Don't automatically assume that first impulsive thought is reality.

Depression may be wrapped around a poor self-view. "I feel insignificant, worthless even." Feelings have to yield to God's truth. He has declared me to be of infinite worth. Do I place my judgment above His? No matter what I think of me, He is the judge. And He has said I am His child.

Depression also is wrought by feeling unworthy of love. "I don't love me, so I don't see how others could either." Again, God, the source of all love, has pronounced me lovable. Am I more psychologically attuned to me than He is? Should I argue with Him: "I think You missed it where I'm concerned"? Believing God's judgment superior to my own is a giant step toward a better mood.

Perhaps you grapple with doubts of incompetence—as a parent, spouse, Christian. Others look to you to be more capable, saintlier. By comparison, you're nagged by the sense that you fall short. In many ways, you don't think you measure up. (A common piece of misthinking.)

God doesn't grade on a curve. He is not about to fail anyone because she isn't in the upper 30 percent in parenting, marriage, or saintliness. Our achievements or competence have little—sometimes nothing—to do with our connection to Him. If God scored on results, everybody would fail the course.

A man is caught in a flood. As the waters rise he climbs to his roof, beseeching God to save him. A boat passes, "Get in." He replies with aplomb, "God will save me." Minutes later a second boat, "Hurry. Climb in. The waters are only going to get higher." Again, "God is watching over me." As he clings precariously to his roof's peak, a helicopter drops a harness. He waves it off, knowing "God will save me." The flood doesn't cooperate, and he is washed off his roof. In heaven he addresses God: "I thought for sure you

Thinking Like Jesus

would save me." God replies, "What did you want? I sent two boats and a helicopter."

Faith is at its strongest when we cooperate with it. Pray for more faith, but pray also for an eternal perspective, better thinking, more insight, more wisdom. And God will send it, perhaps via two boats and a helicopter.

Pray too for an ongoing, ever growing sense of gratitude. The saying is, "It's harder to be depressed when you're grateful." Gratitude and discontent are enemies. Turn your thoughts toward what is going right. You'll have less headroom for what is going wrong.

If your faith rivals those of God's holiest people, you can indeed find peace in the midst of upheaval. As St. Paul writes, "For I have learned, in whatever state I am, to be content" (Phil. 4:11). Notice the "I have learned"? The process is ongoing. If you're anything like I am, or pretty much every one of Christ's followers, your faith is imperfect (read: "weak"). Christ puts faith in perspective. "If you have faith as a grain of a mustard seed, you will say to this mountain, 'Move from hence to yonder place,' and it will move" (Matt. 17:20). My faith sometimes has trouble just moving *me* from here to there.

Putting more trust in God's providence will lighten one's mood. The error lies in thinking the converse—that incomplete faith darkens one's mood. To chastise oneself for weak faith leading to depression is to misunderstand what faith is. It is also to misunderstand what depression is.

30

Self-Projection

Sigmund Freud has been dubbed the father of modern psychiatry. Trained as a neurologist, he fashioned some of the earliest theories on the workings of the human psyche. He lived during the late nineteenth and early twentieth centuries in Austria, and his ideas were shaped somewhat by the sexual attitudes and mores of his time.

Freud divided the personality into several contending parts:

1. The *id*: the seat of one's baser instincts, a seething cauldron of primarily aggressive and sexual impulses. In it resides the passions.

2. The *ego*: the rational negotiator orchestrating compromises between the urges of the id and reality's rules and expectations.

3. The *superego*: one's moral structure, akin to what is now called conscience.

Freud saw people as plagued by repressed psychosexual defects, so he designed an approach to remedy them—psychoanalysis. A mainstay of psychoanalysis is free association. The patient—as they were called in those days—would disclose to a reticent analyst whatever thoughts, urges, and feelings would be percolating in his head. In so doing, the theory went, the concealed conflicts had a route to break through any defenses formed by the ego to protect the patient from his id. Freud called this process "projection." By projecting his psychic strife onto the psychoanalyst, the patient would gain insight into it, thereby moving toward resolution or cure.

Though relatively few therapists still practice psychoanalysis, Freud left his mark in the popular consciousness. Some of his terms have seeped into our everyday language, though with modified meanings. An illustration: A state trooper stopped me for speeding. He asked me about my id. I was just about to ask him, "Were you ever in psychoanalysis?" when I realized he meant my ID.

OK, made-up story. An actual example of Freudian language becoming mainstream is "projection." Originally its meaning was narrow, confined to the patient-analyst relationship. Since, it has projected itself from the office onto everyday relationships. It now means a tendency to be more aware in others of the same faults or motives one possesses.

"Can't she see that she does the very same things she accuses me of?" He says I should watch my language; has he heard his?" "She calls me self-centered; she's one of the most self-centered people I know."

It's universal: We are more attuned to those negatives in others that we have ourselves. What's more, they are often beyond our awareness, lodged somewhere in our "unconscious." Where is that psychoanalyst when I need one?

Projection can be a path to self-insight, though not only as Freud thought. Suppose I am hyperalert to anyone's bragging. It jumps at me quickly and early. That could also mean that I too have a bent toward bragging.

Perhaps I have a sensitive ear for gossip. On one hand, gossip is something I've worked to purge from my conversation, so I've become more vigilant to its mischief. On the other, I too indulge in gossip, mostly unaware. It is always lurking around the next topic of talk.

Freud was right. We have all manner of self-protective ego defenses against coming face-to-face with our own faults. Long before Freud's psychological terminology, Jesus called it a log in one's eye. (see Matt. 7:3). More succinct, and more straightforward.

I can get past my defenses—and my log—by analyzing how I look at others. What I see so easily *in them*, I might do well to look for *in me*. If nothing else, it's a less threatening first step toward self-awareness.

Catholics benefit from the sacrament of Reconciliation not only spiritually but psychologically. Confession requires us to scrutinize ourselves at a deeper level than we'd normally prefer. Without Confession, self-scrutiny could easily atrophy. Unless I am pushed to honestly assess myself, my natural bent is to spend more time assessing others. Do you know anyone who does that?

Projection can shepherd me toward a more insightful confession. When I notice certain sins so easily in others, I can ask myself, "Do I do that? Are those my sins?"

I doubt that Freud ever dreamed that projection could be used to benefit one's soul. (He didn't believe in souls.) However, if being more attuned to the shortcomings of others helps me to analyze my own, then: Sigmund, thank you.

31

The Marriage Test

In graduate school, I learned "assessment." That is, I learned how to use tests to measure just about anything—intelligence, personality, emotions, even test anxiety. We psychologists have constructed an ever-expanding catalogue to measure the highs and lows of the human psyche.

Recently I came across a "marriage test" for husbands. I suspect no professional designed it, so I added a few of my own touches. The test is simple. Be positive and thoughtful toward your wife, and you are awarded points. Be neglectful and self-absorbed, and you are docked points.

For example, you make the bed without being asked—earn 2 points. You are asked more than once—lose 2 points. Tell your preschooler to make it—lose 3 points. Your preschooler makes it better than you do—minus 5 points. To end up in the plus column, volunteer, make it better than a preschooler, and don't take a selfie standing proudly by the bed.

Not to compensate for an earlier tiff, but just because, you bring home a little gift—5 points. You braved the rain for it—2 more. You walk in the house soaked—add 5. The gift is a ratchet set and two rolls of duct tape—all points lost.

Thinking Like Jesus

On your wife's birthday, you make reservations for dinner—10 points. She asks, "Where?" You tease, "It's a surprise"—bonus point. Your surprise is a sports bar—minus 5. And your face is painted in the colors of your favorite team, which just happens to be blaring from all eight TV monitors—minus 50.

You ask your wife if she'd like to leave for someplace quieter and more elegant, allowing for meaningful conversation—plus 15. You're still in the red, but wash off your face in the men's room, and you may break even, barely.

Marriage gurus advise date nights for alone-time togetherness. (This assumes you can find an adolescent willing to babysit the kids for forty bucks an hour plus benefits.) You ask your wife to choose the movie—3 points. It's one she likes, but you don't—3 more. Putting her preferences above yours scores well. She says, "You choose." So you download two tickets to *Rampaging Zombies*—minus 10. You tell her it's a film about poor children who rescue puppies while growing up on a prairie—minus 25. Deception is always a big loser.

Counselors talk incessantly about good communication. In practice, good communication isn't fancy. It begins with a willingness to listen—or, to say it more colloquially, to shut your mouth. For each quiet minute, with no counterarguments, defensiveness, excuses, or accusations, you earn 1 point. As a bonus, you will hear, for better or worse, what matters most to your wife—faith, parenting, in-law relationships, finances, the designated hitter rule in the American League.

You and the television are one as your wife walks in saying, "Can we talk?" Immediately your look conveys, "You mean, can we talk about why I'm frustrated with you?"—minus 10 points. You reply, "About what?"—minus 5. You stare at the TV while your wife is talking—down 5 more. The TV is off the whole time—minus 25.

You turn quietly with a warm look on your face that says, "Go ahead"—plus 5. You ask questions to better understand her reasons for wanting to talk—15 points. You continue to listen, even though you think her reasons are wrong—add 10 points. Not once have you glanced at the television—5 bonus points. Because you've fallen asleep—minus 100.

Scoring high on the marriage test is not complicated: Treat your spouse as Christ would. Scripture nowhere indicates that Jesus took any synagogue psychology courses. As the God-man, He didn't need to. He had an infallible read on human nature. He was the perfect psychologist. When He charged, "Treat others as you wish to be treated," He was giving more than a summary of the moral law. He also knew that others would be moved to respond in kind.

Relationship Law #101 says: The best way to influence someone to treat you better is to treat them better first—no matter how they treat you. The law may not always bring the desired results, everywhere with everyone, but, given enough time, it can move even some of the most resistant souls.

To summarize: The more points you accumulate, the more points will be returned to you. If nothing else, your wife might ask, "Did you take some kind of 'Be-a-better-husband' test?" Five points.

32

Not Feeling It

I navigated graduate school in the '70s. In my counseling classes, feelings were the currency. We identified feelings, shared feelings, accepted feelings, and got in touch with feelings. They were the route to the authentic person and, as such, were given exalted status. While thinking can be misguided and open to logical error, "feelings are neither right nor wrong." So said and still says the modern feelings dictum.

In a scene from a TV sitcom, the wife is upset over her husband's public teasing about her craft project gone awry. Later she expresses, "I felt humiliated." He says that he meant only fun and that she shouldn't feel that way.

"Don't tell me how to feel," she scolds.

"But you're wrong," he counters.

"There is no right or wrong," she re-replies. "That's just how I feel."[4]

Apparently the writers had some counseling courses in college.

---

[4] Steve Skrovan and Ray Romano, "Getting Even," *Everybody Loves Raymond*, season 3, episode 4, directed by Steve Zuckerman, aired October 12, 1998.

Thinking Like Jesus

Since feelings point to the deeper self, to challenge them is considered not only countertherapeutic, but unsympathetic. Even as a rookie psychologist, the heavy priority on feelings left me with, well, a bad feeling.

Before psychology, I was an engineering student. Engineering has absolutes. I couldn't legitimately argue, "Well, you have your formulas, and I have mine." There was no agreeing to disagree. Use the wrong formula, and the bridge will collapse. Engineering principles were cemented in reality. And this fit well with my leanings toward logic and analysis. My emotions, I reasoned, are more fluid. As such, they are not the most reliable guides to right conduct.

The Christian view of the person is more balanced. Certainly feelings are inseparable from who we are. The "heart" is the biblical term used to describe our very core. The heart, however, is not only emotion, but also intellect and will. These trump emotions, as they reflect God's image in us. They are far better counsels to Christlike living, no matter how one might feel.

Is greed wrong? Envy? Resentment? Bitterness? All are feelings. Are they neither right nor wrong, but instead some sort of neutral inner state? Would a husband who feels lust for other women reassure his wife with, "I see my lust as something that is just me. And I need to accept it—so should you—as long as it stays inside and I don't act on it"? In return, she confesses, "I hold a lot of bitterness toward you about that, but don't worry: I've come to realize those feelings are an integral part of my own makeup."

But, goes the argument, as long as one doesn't act on the feelings, where's the wrong? Is hate without retaliation wrong? How about jealousy? Schadenfreude (satisfaction at another's misfortune)? It is intuitive that some feelings by themselves—with no action—help people to live better and some don't.

Further, as the axiom says: The thought gives birth to the feeling gives birth to the action. Feelings percolate when left unchallenged by reason and will. They don't remain idle. They push for expression.

"I can't help how I feel." To answer bluntly, of course you can. It may "feel" as if you can't at the instant of an emotional surge, but the feeling passes or at least lessens in intensity.

More often, a sense of emotional helplessness evolves over time. "I've felt intimidated by my brother-in-law pretty much since the day I met him." "I get so nervous every time I think I might be asked to speak." "My daughter always makes me feel incompetent." "I have to hide my irritation every time he starts in about his accomplishments."

Indeed, if feelings occurred like a reflex, we'd all be impotent victims of them. They'd materialize, and we'd have to live with them until the person or situation provoking them changed. Fortunately, feelings don't live in isolation. They can be created or calmed by our thoughts before, after, and during them. How we understand people's behavior toward us, how we interpret life's fluctuations, how we see ourselves — all heavily influence the way we feel and its resistance to change.

How quickly can a change in interpretation change an emotion? Picture you and me in the middle of an escalating argument. You feel yourself getting hotter by the word. And the feeling seems to be ruling you. Abruptly I slap your cheek. How soon would the feeling erupt? Right after my hand slips off your cheek, no doubt. Your first thought? What's with this guy? Is he crazy? I hope he turns the other cheek so I can slap it.

At one second post slap, were I to ask, "Why are you getting so mad?" You'd likely fire back, "Because you hit me, you jerk." (Or something more colorful?) Immediately, I apologize and point to a hideous spider on the floor. "That jumped from your collar to your cheek."

Thinking Like Jesus

Gripped by your ire, would you get in my face: "I don't care about any spider. You just slapped me, and the more I think about it, the madder I'm getting"? Or would you settle quickly: "Thanks. That thing is ugly, isn't it"?

In fact, I did smack you. But once your perception changed from "You attacked me" to "You protected me," the slap lost its emotional power. You didn't have to choke back some version of, "You're lucky, buddy, that there was a spider on my face right when you hit me." Your anger was instantly replaced by relief or gratitude. The flash feeling dissipated once the slap changed meaning.

"I can't help the way I feel about [person, place, situation]." A sentiment that is routinely voiced in counseling. Were it true, counseling should cease. It would be futile. The day we can no longer reshape our emotions is the day we cease to be alive.

Affording emotions too much life-directing power can rob one of peace. Granted, emotions may fight being controlled or extinguished. That doesn't mean they can't be. The desire to rethink, the will to reconsider, the prayer for help—all are far more involved in shaping character than the ebb and flow of feelings.

"Even if I mouth the right words, I don't feel them." If we waited until we felt like doing good, much good would never get done. One evangelist observed, "How does one reach people who hear with their eyes and think with their feelings?"

Good behavior leads to good habits. Good habits lead to good character. Good character leads to better feelings. That venerable wisdom has been psychologically reversed: One's emotions must show the way before one can "honestly" act that way.

"I don't feel like forgiving; I would be fooling myself." Well, psychologically speaking, it isn't always bad to fool oneself. If forgiveness were primarily a feeling, everybody would be in trouble. Christianity has always taught that forgiveness is first and foremost an act, specifically an act of the will. I decide to forgive. I push myself to release my embrace of the hurtful injustice.

"My will to forgive is weak." A will is weakened by mentally rehearsing the wrong—what happened, how to retaliate, what if it happens again, how many times do I have to forgive? Rehearsal and forgiveness are antagonists. As the inner monologue gains momentum, the willingness to forgive loses momentum. Brooding doesn't give forgiveness any soil in which to root.

A first step to feeling forgiving is to stifle a desire to retaliate. The next: to pray for the offender. It's hard to harbor antagonism toward someone who's getting your prayers. Of course, you may have to first pray for the will to pray.

"I don't feel forgiven." A lament voiced by those who believe that their sin is so wrong or so repetitive that it stretches God's capacity for mercy. Confession routinely doesn't help the feeling, as it lingers afterward. Such feelings are completely irrelevant to the fact of being forgiven. With repentance and the resolve to avoid the sin, *one is forgiven.* How can one be sure? Because God says so. His word is far more trustworthy than our emotions. We have no legitimate right to raise our feelings above God's promise.

Feelings and emotions in our pseudo-therapeutic culture regularly rule over intellect, reason, and will. The Christian view of the person gives emotions their due, but it also understands that good conduct is better guided by right reason and a well-directed will.

33

It's Personal

Not all misinterpretations are equally troublesome. Some create more ire and resentment than others. Topping the list of discord-stoking misunderstandings is what psychologists call "personalizing." This is the inclination to interpret what someone says or does as aimed at oneself. Whatever else might be moving him, it is easy to assume that his main intent is to put down, hurt, or criticize *me*.

A scenario: Walking into the break room at my office suite, I encounter two colleagues talking excitedly with one another. I voice an upbeat, "How's it going?" One answers, "Real good." The other gives me a hard-to-read silent stare. My first thought—straight to that personalizing impulse—is "What's that all about? I don't deserve simple courtesy?"

Walking back to my office, my mind does its own walk. How should I construe the apparent snub? He didn't hear me; he had a family crisis last night; he's a moody guy; the muzak piped into the room was obnoxiously loud. Many possibilities, none personal.

All of which I eliminate. He looked directly back at me; he was laughing, looking not at all distressed; the muzak was setting a positive mood, playing, "Put a Little Love in Your Heart."

Thinking Like Jesus

My first instinct, and my dominant one, is to interpret his silence personally. What did I do to him? Does he dislike me and I never realized it? Do I hold opinions about life, politics, or religion that he can't tolerate? Were they talking me down when I walked in? Whatever, I am convinced the likeliest explanation has something to do with *me*.

Parents routinely couch their discipline in, "I love you, but I don't like what you did." They reassure little Spike that their intent is to teach, not to demean him. Instinctively they understand that the pull to personalize begins young.

Some parents are tormented over their adult child's irresponsibility, immorality, or abandonment of the Faith. They watch as their nineteen-, or twenty-five-, or thirty-one-year-old jettisons the values of his childhood and family. Mixed with their confusion and distress is a load of self-blame. They assume that their child's behavior is directed *at them*, specifically their inadequacies as parents. They not only feel disappointed but unappreciated—a potent combination for emotional distance on both sides of the generational divide.

The potential for personalizing peaks within close relationships. A wife is feeling belittled over her husband's repeated failure to let her know when he'll be late getting home. With each no-call, she becomes more convinced that her pleas are meaningless. He couldn't care less about her schedule—and, by extension, about her.

The husband pleads guilty to tardiness but denies not caring about her wishes or her. In essence, he says he's wrong, and he's trying to improve, though with spotty success.

If she trusts his confession, she may still feel inconvenienced but not personally devalued. Which explanation would make it harder for her to forgive him: that he has some gaps in his social skills, or that he couldn't care less about her?

It's Personal

As a teen, my son Peter lives to finagle more social perks. After some bout of nonstop negotiating, he manages to move his mother's mind toward his. As a husband with more opinions than sense, I comment, "He really can maneuver to get what he wants."

Surely a benign observation, aimed at Peter and not his mother. She, however, doesn't hear me describing Peter. She hears me describing her: "You're easily flimflammed." While my husband side was obtuse, my psychologist side should have anticipated that some remarks are just asking to be personalized. Unless my psychologist side was also obtuse. I wouldn't rule that out.

A logical progression: The more personally I take another's conduct, the more intense my emotions. The more intense my emotions, the harder to muster up the will to forgive.

To forgive more quickly, personalize less quickly. I mean nothing personal here, but, much of the time, others' behavior toward you has nothing to do with you. It has to do with them. Is she hurting emotionally? Is he threatened by your ability or successes? Does she just want to be contrary? Does he fling around his opinions as cosmological truths? When someone sounds as if he's getting personal, it may be more due to his personality than yours.

What if someone does mean to disparage or impugn you? His intent is to insult. No mixed motives in his mind, no nuance in his words. No doubt, that happens. If so, one question matters most: Is it true? If someone thinks I'm a total jerk, he may feel duty bound to enlighten me. Am I really a total jerk? Or only partly? Or do I sometimes do jerky things? There's a big difference there. Just because someone wants to get down and personal doesn't mean I have to oblige him.

Your cousin bristles at how you vote. He not only disputes your right to vote your conscience and values, but he equates his views with the intelligent way to view the world. Because you disagree, you aren't just incorrect but stupid—case closed.

Now what? You could personalize. How can he think I'm stupid? I ought to show him my degrees and awards, challenge him to an IQ-test competition. Or, you could hear his self-assurance as insecurity and his criticism as a sign of a fragile ego. Who knows what all underlies his style? No matter what, you can be sure of one thing: As someone gets more personal, he gets less credible.

Again, all this measuring of someone's motives is not a psychological exercise or strategy practiced in a therapist's office. It is also good for the soul. The slower you are to personalize and the more willing to see other possibilities, the more readily you can forgive.

34

The Law of Social Entropy

The second law of thermodynamics is the Law of Entropy. It declares: Everything tends toward decay. Iron rusts; bodies age; in time the sun will burn out.

The Law of Entropy governs our physical world, but Christians believe that God's timetable rules over that. Jesus will return long before everything runs down or wears out.

The second law of thermodynamics isn't much on people's minds. It doesn't influence our conduct day to day. It may lie somewhere in a fuzzy memory of Physics 101 or we may have come across the question, but couldn't answer it, on *Jeopardy*.

A similar law, though, is highly relevant to our lives. Call it the Law of Social Entropy. It says that over time we tend to get lazier in showing love to those we love. Compliments are further apart. Manners get sloppier. Apologies come slower. Help is lent with one hand instead of two. "I love you" slips from everyday vocabulary.

This law governs most where it should govern least: with spouses, children, and parents. Understandably, the tendency is to become more relaxed over time with loved ones. We know, and they've known, how we feel. Or they should know by now.

Thinking Like Jesus

We don't mean to slip. It just seems to happen. The Law of Social Entropy intrudes, and it gains momentum unless we actively fight it. And we fight it by active love—that is, charity.

Feed the hungry; clothe the poor; visit the prisoner—these are the basics of Christian charity. Christ lived in a time and place where the basics regularly went unmet; thus, He commanded His followers to meet them. In my immediate world, most have their basic needs well met. How, then, can I better love them? With my words.

I have an abundance of words to share (as evidenced by this book). Someone may not need a warm coat, but he could benefit from some warm words—concern, appreciation, admiration, respect. Too often it is these very words that most decay over time.

There is a story of a wife who, throughout thirty years of marriage, pleaded with her husband to tell her, every once in a while, "I love you." He replied, "I told you on our wedding day. If anything changes, I'll let you know."

A priest, during parish missions, challenges the congregation, "Tell your spouse and children that you love them, tonight." He asks why we are slow to say aloud what we know to be true. We assume somehow it will be absorbed by osmosis, through loving acts. He observes, "The words add meaning to the acts."

The priest is blunt: There is absolutely no reason to keep words of love and affection to oneself. They are meant to be given, freely. There are many excuses: "They know I love them." "I'm not an expressive person." "We just never talked that way in my family." "I know I should, but it's not easy for me." "I just don't think about it." Excuses have no place with "I love you." To reverse entropy's trajectory, start with those simple words.

Parents work hard to teach manners. They use the tried-and-trues: "What do you say?" "What's the magic word?" "How do you ask?" Why such effort? Because politeness is more than mere rules of social etiquette. It is a simple way to speak respect. I will be courteous with you because I think you deserve it.

Manners slip as marriages grow more relaxed. Instead of, "Please pour me another cup of coffee.... Thank you," it's "Get me another cup of coffee, would you?" followed by a sipping silence. Rather than "Thanks for turning off the lights," it's "Did you turn off the lights?" The slippage in language is subtle. The message isn't.

Who receives most of your compliments? Those in your life's inner circle, or those on its periphery? Are you quicker with an up-lifting word to a co-worker, a teammate, or a church friend than to a spouse or a child? A client told me he finally realized why he was more positive toward others than toward his wife: He was gathering votes to win the "What a Great Guy" award. He wanted to be liked by many. I wondered: Would his wife vote for him?

Compliments are not verbal tokens, sprinklings of accolades here and there. Nor are they a way to schmooze someone into thinking she's a topnotch person and an elite Christian. A com-pliment is recognized by its sincerity. It says, "I notice you; I appreciate you; I love you." And I want no doubt in your mind about that.

If you've become compliment-careless, try asking, "You know what I like about you?" Or, "You know what I haven't told you in a long time?" You won't hear, "Stop it. I don't need to be flattered. You told me that before." Compliments don't lose meaning by repetition: They gain it.

Put your compliments on paper. Make a list—a long one—of what you like about your spouse. It's a tangible way—and it will be treasured—to say what you may not have said for a long time, or maybe ever. Would your spouse know that you think what you've written?

I made a similar list for my wife. I wrote down all I thought was likeable about me, and then asked her to sign it. She read it over carefully, and then crossed off some items before putting pen to paper.

Of all people, we Christians should be appealing to others—not only in loving action, but in loving words, spoken generously. That will break the Law of Social Entropy.

35

Forced Morals

A television show once invited me as a guest on the topic: "Should parents force their values upon their children, or should they allow them the freedom to choose themselves?" "Force" versus "freedom." Any guess on that show's bias?

Had I felt compelled to accept, I would have asked the host several questions. At what age should a child's freedom to choose begin? Prior to that age, who decides right and wrong? What if the child's chosen morals ruin family peace? If the parents abdicate their moral teaching, who steps in—peers, media, pop culture?

Here's a parenting experiment: As soon as Cookie is old enough to walk and talk, shed all your values and expectations. Lima beans or Twinkies—her pick. Church or television—her vote. Hug her brother or smack him—whatever. She can be kind if she wants, refuse if she wants, go to bed when she wants, visit Grandma when she wants. There will be no compulsion, only freedom designed to shape her into an independent-thinking moral agent.

With every year, is she moving closer to the good and further from the bad? Is she becoming more socialized—a more relatable, rational creature? Or will she regress into a self-absorbed, amoral creature? Almost all parents, and some kids, too, intuitively know the picture would be pretty ugly.

Some experts don't.

A popular parenting program, under its "do's and don'ts" section on savvy communication, advises parents to avoid "moralizing," or telling a child what is right or wrong. The message is that a child needs to form his own morals. He can, but what would they look like?

Parents liberally use "force"—not physical, but social and moral. When beneficial to the child, they make her do what she resists and not do what she desires. Kids are not innately inclined toward acting in their own long-term best interests. (Who is?) If they were, parents wouldn't have to interfere with their decision-making. We could give options, let little Noble pick, and applaud his innate wisdom. The whole growing-up process, for him and us, would be far shorter and smoother.

Self-selected values are even more applauded when they touch upon religion. Teaching clear-cut rights and wrongs, embedded in a religious worldview, is "morally" acceptable so long as a child remains open to it. Should she balk, though, instruction borders on compulsion. Living by this logic, passing on any kind of wisdom—moral or otherwise—would be linked to a child's emotional willingness to agree and cooperate. Supposedly, he would come to see the beauty of grown-up viewpoints on his own.

I'll confess that, as a forward-looking third grader, one who didn't yet know that engineering was ten years in my future, I saw no need to master the multiplication tables. My parents and my teacher required it. Talk about coercion.

Once it was thought to be universal: The lead generation passed morals on to the next. Not everyone agreed about what exactly should be passed on, but all agreed that the older had the duty and experience to do it best. Allowing children to sift through diverse moral selections, picking and choosing which would suit their immediate desires, would have been ridiculed. It wouldn't even be open to discussion, at least until afternoon talk TV.

Those who propose this kind of juvenile liberty, I would think, would have to admit that it would best apply to the second half of childhood. What about the first half? No expert would advise (at least none I've heard) that parents take a passive role in allowing preschool Patty to mold her own conscience. One would have to ignore all that's known about development, intellect, and emotions. Then too, once she is "old enough" (when is that?), what moral structure would she have to build upon? What if early bad moves set a path for more bad moves, in a sort of downward moral spiral? Even were a child given the latitude to shape his own morals, how handicapped and limited would he be by his younger, less informed decisions?

One might disagree with what a parent teaches; this assumption likely lurked in the agenda of the television show that called me. Still, parents have the first right to teach. Do some parents teach so poorly that a child could do better himself? Unfortunately, yes. But some do grow up to make more mature moral choices than their parents ever did.

The journalist Malcom Muggeridge observed, "We have educated ourselves into imbecility." Self-taught morals seem a clear example of Muggeridge's point. It has the sound of educated enlightenment, but how smart is it in reality?

35

Close the Book

Life Law #102: Those who upset us do so regularly. They seem to have the ability to repeatedly rile us. Infrequent offense is easier to overlook; it fades within the overall picture of a relationship. It's the recurrent offenses that test our emotional stamina—and our forgiveness.

"My mother-in-law has been making remarks about my parenting under her breath since our first child. And I can't count how many times she's rolled her eyes." "My boss always has to be right about everything—religion, politics, sports, lawn mowers." "My friend brags constantly about her kids, her house, her cat. I'm ready to scream, 'Stop it! You're obnoxious!'"

Relatively few people—family members, close friends, co-workers—account for the primary strain on our moods. No surprise, as they live inside our life's inner circle. The crabby mail carrier isn't so much a bother, no matter how crabby. Any contact with him is under five minutes a week. And we can always slink out to the mailbox once he's down the street. But we can't avoid those who occupy our nearby world so easily.

I hear it often: "My [name here] makes me so mad when she says [snarky remark]." How long has she been saying [snarky remark]?

"Pretty much ever since I've known her." How long is that? "Twenty-three years." How many more years will you need to conclude that's just what she does? "That may be what she does, but I don't have to like it or tolerate it." You don't have to like it, but you *may* have to tolerate it. Years of evidence make it clear that you may have little choice, short of ending the relationship. And that's extreme, especially if the hard-to-tolerate one is a spouse, parent, grown child, sibling, or in-law.

A qualifier: Because someone can be opinionated, or difficult, or haughty, or critical, it does not follow: He's an idiot; she's a witch; he's a jerk; she's a loser. Because someone acts badly toward me doesn't mean "He's a bad person." Our Father doesn't allow me to so generalize.

Sometime after each affront (an hour, a day, a month?) we talk ourselves down, knowing we should let it go. And with two steps forward, one step back, we regroup—until it happens again. Once more, the same feelings reemerge, stronger, due to the accumulation of history. "When will he see himself as he truly is? Why does she always act like that? Is he ever going to change? How long do I have to put up with this?"

What are your options? Unload your hidden feelings? Throw some verbal punches? Respond in unkind? These are standard "clear the air" strategies. But their standard outcome doesn't clear the air; it only further clouds it.

First of all, a difficult person doesn't usually see himself as difficult. A lack of self-awareness is part of the reason he's difficult. Therefore, his first reaction to being "enlightened" by another will be surprise (Are you talking to me?), followed by denial (That's not me), or defensiveness (Who are you to talk?). The unflattering labels earned by difficult people—thoughtless, abrasive, arrogant, mean-spirited—are not something someone will easily admit to. They are too broad and too personal. Some might acknowledge a piece or two of nasty conduct, but not to being a nasty person.

Should you choose to have a face-to-face encounter, stay away from trait language. Stay particular: "Last Tuesday at 8:22 p.m., you said ... I have it here in my diary, along with a video commentary." OK, maybe not that specific, but you get the idea. Vague accusations resolve little and risk provoking more difficulty.

Is there a better way to bring peace? Yes, call it, "Close the book." Does this mean: end all contact, speak only when spoken to, create a list of excuses to stay away, stop reading this chapter? Not at all. Instead, it means: Stop wanting the person to change. Realize who he is, how he talks, how he acts—yesterday, today, and, in all likelihood, tomorrow. "Close the book" means writing yourself a mental memo: This is how it is.

Will this render you a social doormat? Quite the opposite. It will make you more emotionally steady. You won't have to work so hard to get past the same frustrations every time you're treated as you've been treated in the past. Changing someone who does not want to change is not in your power. Changing you is.

To be sure, the Holy Spirit does have the power to change anyone. And He can use your prayers to do so. Don't close the book on those.

Closing the book of your own frustration lessens recurring ill will. And with less ill will comes more will to forgive. That's the ultimate aim.

About the Author

Dr. Ray Guarendi is a Catholic husband and father of ten adopted children, a clinical psychologist, author, professional speaker, and national radio and television host. His radio show, *The Dr. Is In*, can be heard on the EWTN Global Catholic Radio Network on over 350 stations and Sirius XM (channel 130). His TV show, *Living Right with Dr. Ray*, can be seen on EWTN television, reaching more than 275 million homes in 145 countries and territories.